D1345975

THE VICTORIAN CRISIS OF FAITH

THE VICTORIAN CRISIS OF FAITH

SIX
LECTURES BY

Robert M. Young
Geoffrey Best
Max Warren
David Newsome
Owen Chadwick
R.C.D. Jasper

EDITED BY

Anthony Symondson

PUBLISHED
IN ASSOCIATION WITH THE
VICTORIAN SOCIETY

LONDON
S·P·C·K
1970

First published in 1970
by S.P.C.K.
Holy Trinity Church
Marylebone Road
London N.W.1

Printed in Great Britain by
The Camelot Press Ltd., London and Southampton

SBN 281 02358 1

CONTENTS

CONTRIBUTORS

Anthony Symondson is a member of the committee of the Victorian Society and arranged this course of lectures.

Dr Robert M. Young is a Fellow and Tutor of King's College Cambridge and University Assistant Lecturer in the History of Science.

Geoffrey Best is Professor of Modern History in the University of Edinburgh.

The Reverend Dr Max Warren is a Canon of Westminster Abbey and was General Secretary of the Church Missionary Society from 1942 to 1963.

David Newsome is a Fellow, and Senior Tutor, of Emmanuel College, Cambridge, University Lecturer in Divinity, and Headmaster-designate of Christ's Hospital.

The Reverend Dr Owen Chadwick is Master of Selwyn College and Regius Professor of Modern History in the University of Cambridge.

The Reverend Dr R. C. D. Jasper is a Canon of Westminster Abbey and Chairman of the Church of England Liturgical Commission.

ILLUSTRATIONS

All the illustrations, with the exception of numbers 5 and 8, are reproduced by permission of the National Portrait Gallery.

Note on Illustration No. 8. Westminster Abbey began popular evening services in 1858. They attracted large congregations, for whom gas lighting was specially installed. The psalms which the congregation had to sing were written on pieces of calico and hung from the piers of the nave.

PREFACE

The lectures that form this book were given in a series organized by the Victorian Society at the National Portrait Gallery in the winter of 1968. They were the second series to be held there: and, by the courtesy of the Director, Dr Roy Strong, they now form an annual event. Most of the lectures were accompanied by portraits from the Gallery. It is, therefore, appropriate that some of them have been used as illustrations. The lecturers have given valuable guidance in the choice of subjects; but I am particularly indebted to the Assistant Keeper, Mr Richard Ormond, for his admirable selection from the best available portraits. They are reproduced by permission of the Trustees of the National Portrait Gallery. The engraving of the special Sunday evening service, held in Westminster Abbey in March 1861, is reproduced by permission of the editor of the *Illustrated London News*.

The Victorian Society is the national society responsible for the study and protection of Victorian and Edwardian architecture and other arts. But it should not be regarded as a body whose purpose is confined solely to the study of the history of art, nor exclusively to the preservation and conservation of nineteenth- and early twentieth-century architecture. The Society, as these lectures show, is concerned with the study and appreciation of the entire conspectus of Victorian and Edwardian life. Aesthetic themes are absent from these lectures. They embrace, instead, science, theology, philosophy, politics, and social history. The fabric of Victorian life is examined in relation to one of its most powerful forces, that of religious conviction at variance with scientific discovery and political pressure. The subjects of some of the Society's recent conferences and lectures have equally been concerned with social history, music, and literature. The Victorian Society provides as much for those not interested in architecture and the decorative arts, as it does for those who are.

It is particularly apt that the lectures should be published by the Society for Promoting Christian Knowledge. Dr W. K. Lowther Clarke's book *A History of the S.P.C.K.*, published in 1959, shows how deeply the Society was embedded in the life of the Victorian Church. It was active in the publication and distribution on an immense scale of Bibles, Prayer Books, tracts, religious books, and general literature, many of which were published in foreign languages for use in the mission field. As important as the Society's missionary work was its powerful influence on education, both before and after that responsibility was almost exclusively borne by the Church. Dr Clarke's book includes events that are developed in detail in the lectures. The chapters on the nineteenth century form an instructive companion to this book.

I am deeply grateful to the present staff of the S.P.C.K. for their patience, co-operation, and advice during the preparation for publication.

35 St Andrew's Hill,
E.C.4.
January 1970

ANTHONY SYMONDSON

1

The Impact of Darwin on Conventional Thought

ROBERT M. YOUNG*

The most dramatic confrontation between religion and science occurred in the nineteenth century, and the Christian community remains uneasy about the problem of man's place in nature which became so acute in the Darwinian debate. Recent books on evolution and theology spend more time on the opposition to Darwin and on ways of undermining or getting round the theory than on absorbing and interpreting it. This brief account of the nineteenth-century controversy is aimed at broadening the perspective within which the challenge of Victorian science is viewed and at drawing attention to the views of some members of the Victorian intelligentsia. It is true that the effect of scientific naturalism was to engender a conflict, but Christians are supposed to be primarily concerned with motives and intentions, and the scientists whose views most troubled the Victorian orthodoxy were far from wishing to demean God and man.

When Victoria ascended the throne in 1837, Charles Darwin had recently returned from a six-year, 40,000 mile voyage round the world, puzzled by the question of whether or not species are mutable. In the same year he began a series of notebooks on the species question, which led to the formulation of a theory in 1838, which was not made public for twenty years, i.e., a hundred years before the founding of the Victorian Society. But it is not Darwin's theory by itself or only events after 1837 which have led this Society

* I should like to thank Jeremy Mulford and Joanna Ryan for their most helpful criticisms of an earlier draft of this essay.

to include a talk on evolution in this series. Darwin's theory and its reception were part of a much larger debate on evolution itself, and more generally on a naturalistic or scientific approach to the earth, life, man, his mind, and society which cannot be considered even in relative isolation as starting later than the 1790s.

My first point is, therefore, that Darwin and Darwinism have become clichés for a much wider movement which I shall try to characterize. If we can define its beginning at all, it starts with the publication in 1794–6 of Erasmus Darwin's *Zoonomia.* (Erasmus Darwin was Charles' grandfather, and he put forward a theory of evolution based on David Hartley's psychological theory of associationism in a series of works at the turn of the century.) The image of nature which pervaded his work and that of most naturalists and natural theologians received a heavy blow in 1798 with the appearance of Thomas Malthus' *Essay on the Principle of Population, as it affects the future improvement of society, with remarks on the speculations of Mr Godwin, M. Condorcet, and other writers*, a work which many thought "spread a gloom over the hopes and more sanguine speculations of man" and "cast a slur upon the face of nature".[1] It has been said that Malthus raised a spectre which haunted half the century and that it overshadowed and darkened all English life.[2] Malthus argued that nature's harmony was not perfect; the benevolence of both God and man were called into question. God would not provide food for all the mouths but more than enough mouths for all the food; charity—either private or state—would worsen the lot of the poor. The impact of Malthus' theory was heightened by its apparent mathematical force; in successive generations population could be increased geometrically (2, 4, 8, 16, 32, 64, 128) while in the same time food supplies could only be increased arithmetically (1, 2, 3, 4, 5, 6, 7). The difference between 128 mouths and food for seven represented a potential gulf between unrestrained population growth and man's efforts to provide food. Not only was nature niggardly, but vice, misery, war, famine, and death were inevitable consequences of nature's laws, unless man could restrain his sexual appetite. The Malthusian spectre was a direct challenge to the harmonious image of nature propagated in William Godwin's *Political Justice* (1793), in William Paley's *Natural Theology* (1802), and in the encyclopedia of natural theology which Paley's example inspired—the *Bridgewater Treatises* which appeared in 1833–6, an eleven-volume compendium of the wisdom, goodness, and benevolence of God as manifested in the works of creation. Darwin was to see the Malthusian law of population as a natural law about man, while Alfred Russel Wallace, the co-discoverer of the theory of evolution by natural selection, also found that Malthus provided the essential idea which led him to the theory.

The debate which we summarize by the idea of evolution also embraced the associationist, utilitarian philosophy of the Philosophic Radicals, Bentham, the Mills, and their followers, who would apply natural laws to men and morality and apply sanctions to induce men to act for the greatest good of the greatest number. The pleasures and pains of utilitarian psychological theory became the rewards and punishments of radical reform movements. In effect, Darwin extended this point of view to the ultimate natural sanctions of survival or extinction. One can also say that Darwinism was an extension of *laissez-faire* economic theory from social science to biology. A similar naturalism was at work in the influence of German historical methodology, which suggested that the Bible should be examined *scientifically* like any other historical document.

Another manifestation of the wider movement occurred in geology. The belief in divine interference in nature—in miraculous catastrophic interventions in the course of the history of life and the history of earth—was brought into question by the work of Charles Lyell, whose *Principles of Geology* (1830–3) argued that it was impossible to get on with the actual practice of geological science if one always had to entertain the possibility that the facts were not to be explained by the laws of nature, but that *this* case was a miracle or the result of laws of nature which had ceased to act. How, he asked, could science proceed unless the course of nature in the history of the earth was considered to be uniform, without miraculous catastrophic interventions? Lyell's work led to a debate about the principles and findings of geology in which both sides attempted to be on the side of the angels and at the same time to be true to the principles and data of science. For complex reasons, Lyell argued against evolution but said that, even if it was true, to include man in such a scheme would be to "strain analogy beyond all reasonable bounds".[3] The major evolutionary theorists—Darwin, Chambers, Wallace, and Spencer—all drew heavily on Lyell's work, accepting his principles while rejecting some of their applications: they saw both the history of the earth and the history of life as uniform but, unlike Lyell, considered the history of life to be evolving directionally.

As the so-called "uniformitarian-catastrophist" debate in geology was settling down, there appeared an anonymous work, *Vestiges of the Natural History of Creation*, which argued that it was inconsistent for Lyell to apply the concept of uniform natural laws to the history of the earth and not to the history of life. Similarly, the author drew on another naturalistic tradition about man and animals and argued that phrenology showed that the principle of the uniformity of nature should extend to man and to his mind and brain. Although the name of the author of this work—Robert Chambers—was not made public until 1884 (the speculation attributed it variously to Thackeray, Lady Lovelace, Sir Charles Lyell, George Combe, and Prince Albert), the meaning of his doctrine was quite explicit. Chambers argued that all of nature was under the domain of natural law. He particularly scandalized his readers by saying that man and his mind are governed by natural laws. This was not a novel thesis, but the presentation of the argument for a popular audience caused a great stir.

This same point of view was eloquently expounded in the works of the Professor of Geometry at Oxford, Baden Powell (father of the founder of the Scout Movement), but his works were read only by the intelligentsia. Chambers' *Vestiges of Creation*, on the other hand, sold over 25,000 copies in Britain before 1860, and the phrenological work of George Combe on which it drew for its views on man sold 50,000 copies between 1835 and 1838 and was selling at the rate of 2,500 copies a year in 1843. By the end of the century, according to A. R. Wallace, it had sold 100,000.[4] By comparison Darwin's *Origin of Species*—a scientific best seller—had sold 16,000 copies by 1876 and 47,000 by 1895. Lyell's *Principles* went through editions of 2,000 copies each at a relatively leisurely rate. I do not wish to develop this point further except to reiterate that the impact usually associated with Darwin, Spencer, Wallace, Huxley, *Essays and Reviews*, and John Tyndall, was part of a larger movement embracing a number of naturalistic approaches to the earth, life, and man—in utilitarianism, in population theory, in geology, phrenology, psychology, and in theology itself.

It may be helpful to review the traditional account before examining the intentions of the evolutionists and suggesting a different interpretation of certain aspects of the debate on man's place in nature. The response of conventional belief to Darwin's evolutionism was one which is evoked by the term "impact". Although there had been major controversies over Lyell's geological theory and Chambers' evolutionism, Darwin's scientifically reputable argument came as a weightier blow. The reaction was shock, followed by vehement retaliation. It was felt that the whole edifice of traditional social, ethical, and theological values was at stake. "The

Origin of Species came into the theological world like a plough into an ant-hill. Everywhere those rudely awakened from their old comfort and repose swarmed forth angry and confused."[5] It is not the case that all their replies were incoherent: many were eloquent. However, most of them lacked subtlety; they had no fine texture. Evolutionism was seen as a crude doctrine, and many of the replies were themselves crude. It is, of course, very entertaining to recall this aspect of the Victorian controversy. It is so characteristically Victorian and comes across in a way which leads us to feel reassured that we are much more sophisticated and enlightened. After paying due homage to this pastime, however, it may be worth while to look elsewhere.

Large claims have been made about the influence of evolutionary theory. Here are three examples from the writings of historians: "I myself have little doubt that in England it was geology and the theory of evolution that changed us from a Christian to a pagan nation"[6] ". . . no *rapprochement* was possible between Darwinism as such and protestantism as such. The conceptions of Man were too divergent."[7] "If we may estimate the importance of an idea by the change of thought which it effects, this idea of [evolution by] natural selection is unquestionably the most important that has ever been conceived by the mind of man."[8]

One could indeed tell a chilling tale about the theory of evolution in its various forms as the greatest single blow to man's self-esteem, a tale which rests on the fact that evolution includes mind in the course of natural law. I shall spend some space sketching it, using quotations which convey the quality of the impact. As the theory was put by Robert Chambers (who had the good sense to remain anonymous) in 1844, "It is hardly necessary to say, much less to argue, that mental action, being proved to be under law, passes at once into the category of natural things. Its old metaphysical character vanishes in a moment, and the distinction usually taken between physical and moral is annulled."[9] It was this conclusion which produced apoplectic responses. For example, Adam Sedgwick wrote a scathing review of the book and shows himself even more upset in a letter to Charles Lyell. He wrote of Chambers,

> I do from my soul abhor the sentiments [of the book] and I believe I could have crushed the book by proving it base, vulgar in spirit, . . . false, shallow, worthless, . . . And what shall we say to his morality and his conscience, when he tells us he has "destroyed all distinction between moral and physical"; when he makes sin a mere organic misfortune? . . . If the book be true, the labours of sober induction are in vain; religion is a lie; human law is a mass of folly,

> and a base injustice; morality is moonshine; our labours for the black people of Africa were the works of madmen; and man and woman are only better beasts! When I read some pages of the foul book, it brought Swift's satire to my mind, and filled me with such inexpressible disgust that I threw it down. . . .[10]

Not content with an eighty-five page tirade in the *Edinburgh Review* for 1845,[11] Sedgwick added further remarks to a new edition of a modest pamphlet on the *Studies of the University of Cambridge*, a work of some ninety-four pages plus notes. Sedgwick added a preface of 450 pages and a supplementary appendix which added a further 150. These contained a sustained attack on Chambers' version of evolution, as the main target, but it was (I think rightly) associated with strong criticisms of the dangerous doctrines of phrenology, German biblical criticism, Tract 90, and the utilitarian theory of morals along with its foundations in the philosophy of Locke.[12]

Sedgwick was no crank. Indeed, he was Professor of Geology at Cambridge, and, at various times, President of the Geological Society, a Fellow of the Royal Society, President of the British Association in 1833 and of its Geological Section many times. He was thus a respected scientist reacting against an evolutionary theory and its application to man and to mind. His own geological position, however, was at least two removes from more extreme theological opinion. In 1831 Sedgwick had criticized those who had attempted to argue that geological evidence supported a fairly literal reading of Genesis on the Flood.[13] Foremost among those who had tried to find geological evidences for the Mosaic Flood was William Buckland, Professor of Mineralogy and of Geology at Oxford before he became Dean of Westminster. However, Buckland, in turn, was attempting to interpret scripture less literally than others.[14] For example, when the British Association went to York in 1844, William Cockburn, Dean of York, criticized both Sedgwick and Buckland and urged that the whole of the evidence of geology supported the traditional chronology and the literal interpretation of Genesis. At the beginning of the pamphlet which Cockburn published giving his account of the controversy, he quotes the following lines from Cowper:

> Some drill and bore
> The solid earth and from the strata there
> Extract a register, by which we learn
> That He who made it and revealed its date
> To Moses, was mistaken in its age.[15]

It is symptomatic of the separation of such views from those of informed and Christian scientists that Cockburn's letters to Sedgwick and to the Geological Society were met with polite but unencouraging replies. Cockburn took this to mean that he had won the day and wrote to his flock as the meeting of the British Association broke up, "My dear Fellow-Citizens, The philosophers are going. We may I think congratulate each other that during their much feared visitation among us they have certainly not established any one fact which would weaken our faith in the Sacred historians [of the Bible]."[16] I remind you that Cockburn's opponent, Buckland, was the most nearly literalist of the professional geologists. Even so, Cockburn found his geology too risky and said this of Buckland's work:

> Oh Oxford! so long the seat of learning, religion, and orthodoxy—who could have believed that out of thee should come a cherished voice leading the children committed to thy care directly to infidelity and indirectly to atheism?[17]

Taking this same account further, one could point to the effect of Darwin's one modest sentence on man in the *Origin of Species*. He said, and this was a somewhat reluctant gesture, merely this: "Light will be thrown on the origin of man and his history."[18] This produced a classic confrontation between Samuel Wilberforce and T. H. Huxley at the meeting of the British Association at Oxford in 1860.[19] Wilberforce also attacked Darwin in writing in a way which was reminiscent of Sedgwick's attack on Chambers' *Vestiges*. After noting that Darwin would apply "his scheme of the action of the principle of natural selection to MAN himself, as well as to the animals around him", Wilberforce continues,

> Now, we must say at once, and openly, that such a notion is absolutely incompatible not only with single expressions in the word of God on that subject of natural science with which it is not immediately concerned, but, which in our judgment is of far more importance, with the whole representation of that moral and spiritual condition of man which is its proper subject-matter. Man's derived supremacy over the earth; man's power of articulate speech; man's gift of reason; man's free will and responsibility; man's fall and man's redemption; the incarnation of the Eternal Son; the indwelling of the Eternal Spirit, —all are equally and utterly irreconcilable with the degrading notion of the brute origin of him who was created in the image of God, and redeemed by the Eternal Son assuming to himself his nature.[20]

Wilberforce goes on to condemn Darwin's view of the future

development of man and to dismiss the claim that the theory of evolution leads to a grander view of the Creator.

A further symptom of the confrontation of the naturalist interpretation of the history of life, of the earth, and of the scriptures themselves, occurred in 1860, when *Essays and Reviews* defended empirical methods as the legitimate means of investigating anything at all. The Bible was seen as a document written by men; its relevance was moral, it had limitations deriving the period when it was written, and it was decidedly not about geology or biology. The reaction to *Essays and Reviews* showed just how much was at stake when naturalist explanations were advocated in sensitive areas.[21] To continue this account along traditional lines, the next stage is John Tyndall's Presidential Address in 1874 to the Meeting of the British Association at Belfast, in which he claims that science has an unrestricted right to investigate all of nature. This provoked a storm of controversy for the usual reasons.[22] Of course, the final and most entertaining confrontation between evolutionism and the scientific method on the one hand and traditional opinion on the other is contained in the brilliant polemical essays of T. H. Huxley, nine volumes of wit and venom all aimed at opposing naturalism to traditional views of nature and man. When the story arrives at Huxley, the futility of pursuing it further becomes apparent, for we have heard it all before. So much is he the subject of incantation that a selection of his writings, arranged by topic, has recently appeared.[23] The scientist and free-thinker can now use Huxley handily for any suitable occasion: the thoughts of "Darwin's Bulldog" to put alongside those of Chairman Mao.

So far I have said that the reinterpretation of man's place in nature was not primarily due to the work of Darwin but involved a more general debate and that the impact on conventional belief did not involve anything which has not been said many times before. One more thing should be said before turning to the positive side. It is that the objections made sense. The separation of mind and free will from the course of material nature lies at the bottom of our traditional idea of responsibility and of the spiritual aspect of man. Thus it seemed that our systems of morality and of law, as well as of the hopes and punishments of man, were at stake. Similarly, banishing miracles appeared to call into question the divine origin of the earth and of man as well as the Incarnation and Resurrection, i.e. the indispensable underpinnings of the Christian faith. As John Henry Newman once said, it would not pay the Church to break silence on the Mosaic flood, if this question would also lead men to doubt the Incarnation.[24] The extraordinary interest in evolution thus arose naturally from the union which the theory implied between man's spiritual nature and his body, particularly his nervous system (territory over which Huxley and Owen fought in the 1860s).[25] Man's body was his animal nature, and this connection gave him a stake in the question of how animal types came to be: the history of life was invested with theological meaning. If it had occurred through struggle and famine, what of God's concern for the fall of a sparrow? From life one naturally moves to the stage on which it occurs, the Earth. The origin and history of the Earth is thus of theological interest. One does not need to rely on questions about the literal time-scale implied by counting generations from Adam and Eve, to become worried about developments in geology and biology: the issue is much more general. Does the origin of the earth have a higher meaning? Was there a moral convenant between God and man and a later redemption? Few were as simple-minded as Cockburn, but many saw that the exclusion of all non-material causes from nature did not merely eliminate miracles from Genesis. It threatened the status of mind and will and the hope for a moral meaning to life outside of life itself.

In what follows I do not wish to imply that I do not think that there is a conflict between the implications of evolution and Christian beliefs. I think that there is a fundamental conflict centring on the relationship of the mind and the brain and that science cannot sanction a metaphysic which allows any forces or events which transcend the continuity of nature or natural laws. What I want to emphasize, however, is that the idea of opposing theology could not have been further from the minds of the main evolutionists. Their aim was to reconcile nature, God, and man. Putting the issue very crudely, there are three possible ways of characterizing the relationship between science and theology. First, that of traditional natural theology up to the *Bridgewater Treatises* claims that each new discovery of science is a separate additional proof of the wisdom, power, and goodness of the Deity. Thus science, though separate from revelation, complements it. Second, at the other extreme, is the view that each new discovery of science diminishes the domain of theological interpretation. If the Genesis story is false, the Biblical account of creation and of man's spiritual nature is in doubt. If there have been no geological catastrophes outside the course of natural laws (especially the Mosaic flood), then all miracles are in doubt. If man is an animal, and the brain is the organ of the mind, then free will and responsibility are on shaky ground. The role of non-material causes, whether they be miracles or acts of mental effort, is progressively diminished. The advance of science does not confirm theology, it refutes it. I want to argue that the period from about 1820 to 1875 was one in which science made it clear to enlightened theological opinion that a third interpretation of the relationship between science and theology was necessary. One could argue that this was not a novel synthesis—that this change was really an advance on the part of theology, or that it implied that where science advanced, theology (therefore God) retreated. Advocates of the "new" natural theology said that it involved a grander view of the Creator, while the more literal-minded interpreters of the scriptures and the more evangelical ministers attempted an increasingly unsuccessful holding action. The natural theology which began to emerge in the 1840s said, quite simply, that one of the traditional tasks of natural theology—theodicy, or the justification of the ways of God to man—could not be undertaken with the assurance and at the level which had prevailed in the works of John Ray, Bishop Butler, or William Paley. As William Whewell, the Lord Chancellor of scientific controversy in this period put it, theology can gain nothing but lose much by teaching science as the proof of scripture. When a scientific finding conflicts with a passage in scripture, we must find a new way of understanding the passage in question.[26]

The most nearly consistent exponent of the natural theology of the evolutionists was Baden Powell, who argued that science should not even be juxtaposed with scripture: they were bound to conflict. He went further and reminded his readers that the book of God's works was separate from the book of God's words. So insistent was he that they should not be mingled that he claimed that moral and physical phenomena were completely independent. Powell was the philosopher of almost complete faith in the uniformity of nature (except, note particularly, man's mind), and it is interesting to find him writing his most significant works as a succession of defences, first of Lyell's uniformitarian geology; next of Chambers' theory of evolution—uniform laws applied to the history of life, including man; and just before he died, in his contribution to *Essays and Reviews*, he said, "a work has now appeared by a naturalist of the most acknowledged authority, Mr Darwin's masterly volume on *The Origin of Species* by the law of 'natural selection',—which now substantiates on undeniable grounds the very principle so long denounced by the first naturalists,—*the origination of new species by natural causes*: a work which must soon bring about an entire revolution of opinion in favour of the grand principle of the self-evolving powers of nature".[27]

I do not believe that these developments were unconnected with the progressive polarization of the debate. Very roughly speaking, as the period proceeds, one must look to less and less informed and intelligent men for literal interpretations of the Bible. As early as 1819 the *Quarterly Review* was already ridiculing an overzealous attempt to subordinate geological facts to the Genesis account and to describe the flood as punishment.[28] When the British Association went to York in 1844, Dean Cockburn's attempt to correct Buckland's geology, to include all of geological history within 6,000 years, and to reconcile geological findings with a fairly literal interpretation of the Genesis account, was simply an embarrassment to the President of the Association, the President of the Geological Society, and to Adam Sedgwick.[29] A similar encounter at Oxford in 1860 did no credit to Bishop Wilberforce, nor did his rude and presumptuously patronizing review of the *Origin of Species* in the *Quarterly Review*.[30] Similarly in the later part of the century and beyond, the debate was characterized as completely polarized. There are titles such as *The Conflict between Religion and Science*, *A History of the Warfare of Science with Theology*, and *Landmarks in the Struggle between Science and Religion*.[31] The emergence of such works is as unsophisticated a response to the triumph of evolution as the reactions from the earlier period. The only serious study of the reception of evolution makes it apparent that there was no coherent, easily analysable reaction to the theory and its implications.[32] If I am asked about the impact of science and evolutionism on the general public, I find that the reaction was one of unanalytic, total rejection. Darwin was a name to be invoked as a cliché, to be rejected by the faithful, or embraced by the secularists; if, however, I am asked about the impact on the intelligentsia, I find them making a subtle accommodation with the theory and adopting an attendant natural theology which, while it made God more remote from nature, made his rule grander at the same time that it left him much more a personal deity. Finally, I want to reiterate my belief that there is little evidence to show that any of the principal figures in the debate were antitheistic, much less atheistic. By concentrating on Huxley and Tyndall historians have failed to see just how easily the theory of evolution was accommodated by some of the most sophisticated and subtle thinkers of the period.

One can approach this same point another way by arguing that the evolutionary debate was merely a demarcation dispute within natural theology. There is a passage from Sir Francis Bacon's *Advancement of Learning* which helps to make this point. Bacon says,

> . . . let no man, upon a weak conceit of sobriety, or an ill-applied moderation, think or maintain, that a man can search too far, or be too well studied in the book of God's word, or the book of God's works, divinity or philosophy; but rather let men endeavour an endless progress, or proficience in both; only let them beware that they apply both to charity, and not to swelling; to use, and not to ostentation; and again, that they do not unwisely mingle, or confound these learnings together.[33]

Thus, Bacon advocates the diligent study of both the Bible and Nature but warns against confusing them. The point about Bacon's advice is not that it is transparently good advice but that everyone thought that he was following it. That is, scriptural geologists in the 1690s, made the same point as they happily used biblical passages as a substitute for geological investigation, and this mixing of science and the Bible was later offered as a lesson to Buckland. Yet Buckland had quoted Bacon's advice in making his own case for liberalizing literalist geology and at the same time attempting to prove the reality of the Mosaic Deluge. Charles Lyell quoted it as his manifesto in an early geological review which criticized Buckland's views. Baden Powell's writings can be seen as a series of reiterations of Bacon's maxim, expressed *passim* in each of his defences of a uniformly naturalistic view of geology and evolution. Adam Sedgwick quoted Bacon as part of his attack on Chambers for evolutionism. Indeed, Darwin quoted it in the frontispiece of the *Origin of Species.*[34] Each was determined to separate science from theology, but the question was where to draw the line. Many of these people were both Doctors of Divinity and Fellows of the Royal Society. They were trying to reconcile their Genesis with their geology. As Powell put it in 1838,

> Scientific and revealed truth are of essentially *different natures,* and if we attempt to combine and unite them, we are attempting to unite things of a kind which cannot be consolidated, and shall infallibly injure both. In a word, in physical science we must keep strictly to physical induction and demonstration; in religious inquiry, to moral proof; but never confound the two together. When we follow observation and inductive reasoning, our inquiries lead us to *science.* When we obey the authority of the Divine Word, we are not led to *science* but to *faith.* The mistake consists in confounding these two

distinct objects together; and imagining that we are pursuing science when we introduce the authority of revelation. They cannot be combined without losing the distinctive character of both.[35]

The problem was not whether or not God governed the universe, but how. And the answer became, increasingly, "in the manner of law, not by meddling". Chambers put this point particularly well. He asked if God really used special miracles to alter a tooth, or a new tubercle or cusp on the third molar, thus distinguishing one species from another.[36] In the seventeenth century, scientists had been warned not to have recourse to God in explaining the origins of particular things, or to miracles to explain particular effects, and in the mid-nineteenth century geologists and biologists began to see the point.

Looking at the argument this way round, then, the evolutionists were explicitly arguing for a grander view of the Creator. The other two quotations on the frontispiece of the *Origin of Species* are to the effect that God acted once to establish general laws, not by isolated interpositions of divine power. These same sentiments were expressed (again, with varying degrees of conviction) by Lyell, by Sir John Herschel (who thought separate creations reflected an inadequate conception of the creator), by Charles Babbage (the inventor of the computer—who tried to show that apparent miracles were really higher laws), by A. R. Wallace, and so on.[37] The *Origin of Species* is littered with phrases like "far higher workmanship", and "the laws impressed on matter by the creator".[38] Lest it be thought that Darwin used such phrases as a gesture towards public opinion, it is worth mentioning that they also occur in the first pencil sketch of his theory, written for his eyes only in 1842. In the conclusion he wrote,

It accords with what we know of the law impressed on matter by the Creator, that the creation and extinction of forms, like the birth and death of individuals, should be the effect of secondary [laws] means. It is derogatory that the Creator of countless systems of worlds should have created each of the myriads of creeping parasites and [slimy] worms which have swarmed each day of life on land and water on [this] one globe.[39]

Belief in the inviolability of natural causes operating continuously throughout nature was indispensable if science was to be possible. The main works of Darwin, Chambers, and Lyell were all arguments in favour of interpreting nature according to fixed laws. They were not merely reports of scientific discoveries. They were concerned with the principles of reasoning, the assumptions, of science. (Indeed, Spencer once claimed that the law of evolution was an inevitable corollary of belief in natural causation.[40]) They argued that the interests of both science and of theology required that their foundations be considered separately. Each could take care of itself and could only suffer from intermingling. The outcome of the demarcation dispute was that *all* of nature was seen as falling within the domain of law and was the legitimate object of scientific inquiry. This was the burden of John Tyndall's controversial "Belfast Address" in 1874, and of Huxley's most church-baiting remarks. At the same time, however, it could be granted that all of nature was within the domain of God's law. Science laid no claim to the faith of the believer. Even Huxley was not an atheist: he coined the term "agnostic". When Sir Charles Lyell was interred in Westminster Abbey in 1875, A. P. Stanley reflected the growing reconciliation in his funeral oration: "The tranquil triumph of Geology, once thought so dangerous, now so quietly accepted by the Church, no less than by the world, is one more proof of the groundlessness of theological panics in the face of the advances of scientific discovery." Seven years later, in 1882, Charles Darwin was also buried in Westminster Abbey, a few feet from the grave of Sir Isaac Newton. One view of this honour was that it proved that England was no longer a Christian country, while another was expressed by Dean Farrar in his funeral sermon:

> This man, on whom for years bigotry and ignorance poured out their scorn, has been called a materialist. I do not see in all his writings one trace of materialism. I read in every line the healthy, noble, well-balanced wonder of a spirit profoundly reverent, kindled into deepest admiration for the works of God.[41]

Two years after that, Frederick Temple's Bampton Lectures on *The Relations between Religion and Science* included a reassuring chapter on the "Apparent Collision between Religion and the Doctrine of Evolution" which concluded, ". . . we cannot find that Science, in teaching Evolution, has yet asserted anything that is inconsistent with Revelation, unless we assume that Revelation was intended not to teach spiritual truth only, but physical truth also".[42] A quarter of a century before writing this Temple (then Headmaster of Rugby) had been one of the subjects of heated controversy which involved two of his co-authors in prosecutions in theological courts, a storm which led to the Privy Council and the Lord Chancellor. He and the other authors of *Essays and Reviews* were called "septem contra Christum". Twelve years after writing it, Temple became Archbishop of Canterbury.[43]

But what did this leave? Was the whole of the meaning of evolution summed up in one verse?

> There was an ape in days that were earlier;
> Centuries passed and his hair became curlier;
> Centuries more and his thumb gave a twist,
> And he was man and a Positivist.[44]

What had happened to the hopes which had been endangered by science?

Having argued that the evolutionary debate produced an adjustment within a basically theistic view of nature rather than a rejection of theism, I now want to go on to say that what evolution took away from man's spiritual hopes by separating science and theology and making God remote from nature's laws, it gave back in the doctrine of material and social and spiritual progress.

Far from justifying the fears of the more conventional objectors to evolution, the authors of the theory were believers in a most compassionate philosophy which absorbed pain and struggle into a sanguine belief in progress which was as optimistic as the most extreme hopes of the faithful. Belief in progress was not new in the nineteenth-century evolutionists, nor did they have a monopoly of it. They yielded to none in their faith, and their version of the doctrine of unlimited progress had the additional support of being guaranteed by the laws of nature. Lyell, an anti-evolutionist until 1869, had said in his first defence of uniformitarian geology, in 1827,

> If there be no attribute which more peculiarly characterizes man than his capability of progressive improvement, our estimate of the importance of this progressive power is infinitely enhanced by perceiving what an unlimited field of future observations is unfolded to us by geology, and by its various kindred sciences.[45]

If Lyell could say this on the basis of the new geology, how much more could Spencer say in 1857, on the basis of his own theory of evolution (two years before Darwin's theory was published) that progress was not merely a fact about man. In his essay on "Progress: Its Law and Cause", he said,

> It will be seen that as in each phenomenon of to-day, so from the beginning, the decomposition of every expended force into several forces has been perpetually producing a higher complication; that the increase of heterogeneity so brought about is still going on,

and must continue to go on; and that thus Progress is not an accident, not a thing within human control, but a beneficent necessity.[46]

Is this anti-religious? He goes on to say that this does not imply that the great problems of philosophy are solved. "Let none thus deceive themselves. Only such as know not the scope and the limits of Science can fall into so grave an error. After all that has been said, the ultimate mystery of things remains just as it was." Explaining one thing only "brings out into greater clearness the inexplicableness of that which remains behind". . . . "We feel ever more and more certain that fearless inquiry tends continually to give a firmer basis to all true Religion." Absolute knowledge is impossible; under all things lies an impenetrable mystery.[47] Spencer had recovered the eighteenth-century faith that had been rudely challenged by Malthus' attack on the hopes of unlimited perfectibility of Godwin and Condorcet. John Burrow has argued in his excellent work on *Evolution and Society* that this was the main point of embracing evolution: it provided a guarantee of progress, where the utilitarians had only been able to hope that they could engineer it.[48]

In the *Origin of Species*, Darwin mixed his belief in various manifestations of progress with scientific prophecy. If we look at the whole book as a plea to view nature in terms of the principle of the uniformity of nature, the last chapter can be read as Darwin's promise of the fruits which will be ours if we will do so. He says, "When the views entertained in this volume on the origin of species, or when analogous views are generally admitted, we can dimly foresee that there will be a considerable revolution in natural history." But Darwin is a naturalist at heart, and the first fruits he promises are that classification and naming will be less difficult for naturalists. He goes on: "A grand and almost untrodden field of enquiry will be opened, on the causes and laws of variation," and other biological questions. He also mentions benefits to breeders, geologists, and others. In the paragraph which provoked the greatest outcry he maintains the same mode of address: "In the distant future I see open fields for far more important researches. Psychology will be based on a new foundation, that of the necessary acquirement of each mental power and capacity by gradation. Light will be thrown on the origin of man and his history." In the next—the penultimate—paragraph he says,

To my mind it accords better with what we know of the laws impressed on matter by the Creator, that the production and extinction of the past and present inhabitants of the world should have been due to secondary causes, like those determining the birth and death of the individual. When I view all beings not as special creations, . . . they seem to me to become ennobled.

"We can," he says,

so far take a prophetic glance into futurity as to foretel that it will be the common and widely-spread species, belonging to the larger and dominant groups, which will ultimately prevail and procreate new and dominant species. . . . And as natural selection works solely by and for the good of each being, all corporeal and mental endowments will tend to progress towards perfection.

It is interesting to contemplate an entangled bank, clothed with many plants of many kinds, with birds singing on the bushes, with various insects flitting about, and with worms crawling through the damp earth, and to reflect that these elaborately constructed forms, so different from each other, and dependent on each other in so complex a manner, have all been produced by laws acting around us.

He then lists—rather hopefully—the laws and concludes,

Thus, from the war of nature, from famine and death, the most exalted object which we are capable of conceiving, namely, the production of the higher animals, directly follows. There is grandeur in this view of life, with its several powers, having been originally breathed into a few forms or into one; and that, while this planet has gone cycling on according to the fixed laws of gravity, from so simple a beginning endless forms most beautiful and most wonderful have been, and are being, evolved.[49]

Stylistically, this is the place to end, but history is not so tidy. There were at least two advocates of progress by evolution who were even more sanguine. Darwin's belief in progress concentrated on natural history. He wrote more on plants than on animals and more on animals than on man. Spencer was particularly concerned with man, and his belief in progress was unequivocal: the basic motive for his life's work was to place this belief on a secure foundation. Out of the belief in progress through struggle there grew the ideology of so-called "Social Darwinism". This provided the intellectual underpinnings for defences of imperialism in this country and the so-called robber barons in America.[50] This point of view was reflected in Walter Bagehot's *Physics and Politics* and provides another aspect of the impact of evolution on conventional belief.[51] But much depends on one's conventions, and evolutionism also served as a rationale for very different political and social views. Alfred Russell Wallace's belief in progress increased as the years went on and as he became more concerned with social problems. As early as 1864 (only six years after his co-discovery of evolution by means of natural selection) he was ceasing to believe in the all-sufficiency of the mechanism of natural selection where man was concerned. He wrote in 1864 that progress is slow,

> but it still seems to be progress. . . . there is undoubtedly an advance—on the whole a steady and permanent one . . .; and as I cannot impute this in any way to "survival of the fittest," I am forced to conclude that it is due to the inherent progressive power of those glorious qualities which raise us so immeasurably above our fellow animals, and at the same time afford us the surest proof that there are other and higher existences than ourselves, from whom these qualities may have been derived, and towards whom we may ever be tending.[52]

In later years Wallace became almost exclusively absorbed by social problems, and in 1898 he attempted to sum up the successes and failures of *The Wonderful Century*. The appendix of that book is worth examining. It is entitled "The Remedy for Want in the Midst of Wealth". Wallace begins as follows:

> The experience of the whole century, and more especially of the latter half of it, has fully established the fact that, under our present competitive system of capitalistic production and distribution, the continuous increase of wealth in the possession of the capitalist and landowning classes is *not* accompanied by any corresponding diminution of the severity and misery and want or in the numbers of those who suffer from extreme poverty, rendered more unendurable by the presence of the most lavish waste and luxury on every side of them.[53]

And he continues,

> I have done what I can to prove the utter breakdown of our present state of social disorganization—a state which causes all the advances in science and in our command over the forces of nature to be absolutely powerless to check the growth of poverty in our midst. Every attempt to salve or to hide our social ulcers has failed, and must continue to fail, because those ulcers are the necessary product of Competitive Individualism.

He concludes,

> I therefore call upon all earnest and thinking men and women to devote their energies to advocating those more fundamental changes which both theory and experience prove to be needed, and which alone have any chance of success.
>
> For now—though oft mistaken, oft despairing,
> At last, methinks, at last I see the dawn;
> At last, though yet a-faint, the awakening nations
> Proclaim the passing of the night forlorn;

John Collier

CHARLES DARWIN

George Richmond

BISHOP SAMUEL WILBERFORCE

So shall the long-conceived child of Time
Be born of Progress—soon the morn sublime
Shall burst effulgent through the clouds of Earth,
And light Time's greatest page—O Right, thy glorious birth![54]

Lest this seem an irrelevant polemical plea for socialism, or even slightly so, I ought perhaps to remind you that the movement of thought which produced the Darwin–Wallace theory of natural selection also produced (if we interpret it very widely indeed), in 1860, the following remark on Darwin's *Origin of Species*: "although it is developed in the crude English style, this is the book which contains the basis in natural history for our view".[55] Twenty years after Karl Marx wrote this to Freidrich Engels, he wrote to Darwin and asked if the English edition of *Das Kapital* might be dedicated to him. Darwin politely declined, since he had no wish to be associated with attacks on Christianity and Theism.[56]

I did not set out to show that the common assumption of a conflict between theology and science is without foundation. I have only tried to suggest that a desire for conflict was not an important motive in the debate. Also, when the advocates of an evolutionary view did encroach on the domain of theism, they provided an alternative view of man and society which was as sanguine and Utopian in its belief in progress as were the views of the afterlife advocated by the most evangelical, antiscientific, scriptural literalist. Marxism is, of course, the most striking example of a Victorian, this-wordly, utopian philosophy, promising inevitable social progress. In the same period, the author of the extremely popular work, *A History of the Conflict between Religion and Science*, also claimed that social advancement is as completely under the control of natural law as is bodily growth.[57]

In conclusion, I should like to reiterate my main points. "Darwinism" has been made to stand for a much wider naturalistic movement in psychology, social theory, and science and cannot be fruitfully studied in isolation. The effect of its impact on popular opinion was considerable but was characterized by a lack of subtlety which makes a close study of the theological and social views of the intellectual *élite* a much more rewarding enterprise than merely invoking conventional homilies. Finally, the evolutionary debate was seen by its participants as occurring within natural theology, with no antitheistic overtones, while those who used evolution for other purposes were themselves devoted believers in the secular religion of Progress, albeit a different religion, but one which has retained its appeal for the faithful.

NOTES

Throughout this talk I have refrained from mentioning Positivism, since to do so would have made the narrative too complicated. However, if one were to provide a balanced account of the development of scientific naturalism, various adumbrations of the Comtist doctrine would have to be added to pp. 13–16, 27–31, along with a discussion of the impact of Positivism on J. S. Mill, G. H. Lewes, Spencer, and Huxley, along with the expository and polemical works of Harriet Martineau, John Morley, and Frederic Harrison. The temptation to use the positivist movement as an all-embracing umbrella for too many aspects of scientific naturalism has led me to prefer omission to the risk of increased confusion. (*See* Noel Annan, *The Curious Strength of Positivism in English Political Thought* (London, Oxford 1959; Leslie Sklair, "Comte and the Idea of Progress", *Inquiry* 11:321-31, 1968; Edwin N. Everett, *The Party of Humanity* (Chapel Hill, North Carolina 1939), ch. 3; Sydney Eisen, "Frederic Harrison and the Religion of Humanity", *South Atlantic Quart.* 66:574-90, 1967; W. M. Simon, *European Positivism in the Nineteenth Century*, (Ithaca, Cornell 1963).

1. William Hazlitt, "Mr Malthus", in *The Spirit of the Age, or Contemporary Portraits*, 1825. Reprint (London, Oxford 1904), p. 159.
2. Basil Willey, "Origins and Development of the Idea of Progress", in Grisewood, Harman, et al., *Ideas and Beliefs of the Victorians* (1949). Reprint (N.Y., Dutton 1966), p. 43; Humphrey House, "The Mood of Doubt", in ibid., p. 74.
3. Charles Lyell, *Principles of Geology, being an Attempt to Explain the Former Changes of the Earth's Surface by Reference to Causes Now in Operation*, 3 vols. (London, Murray 1830–3), vol. I, p. 156. *cf.* Walter F. Cannon, "The Uniformitarian-Catastrophist Debate", *Isis* 51:38–55, 1960.
4. George Combe, *The Constitution of Man, Considered in Relation to External Objects* (1828), 5th American edn (Boston, Marsh, Capen & Lyon 1835); Leslie Stephen, "George Combe" in *Dictionary of National Biography* (London, Smith, Elder 1887), Vol. XI, p. 428; Alfred R. Wallace, *The Wonderful Century: Its Successes and Failures* (1898), 4th edn. (London, Swan Sonnenschein 1901), p. 164.
5. Leo J. Henkin, *Darwinism in the English Novel, 1860–1910* (1940). Reprint (N.Y., Russell & Russell 1963), p. 62.
6. F. Sherwood Taylor, "Geology Changes the Outlook" in *Ideas and Beliefs of the Victorians*, op. cit., 1966 (see above, note 2), p. 195.
7. John Dillenberger, *Protestant Thought and Natural Science. A Historical Interpretation* (London, Collins 1961), p. 224. See the chapter: "The Darwinian Impact".
8. George J. Romanes, *Darwin, and After Darwin*, 3 vols. (London, Longmans, Green 1892–7), Vol. I, pp. 256–7.
9. [Robert Chambers] *Vestiges of the Natural History of Creation*, 2nd edn. (London, Churchill 1844), pp. 333–4. Cf. 1st edn. (1844), p. 315. This crucial passage is modified in later editions; see 12th edn. (London, Chambers 1884), pp. 373 & lxvii.
10. John W. Clark and Thomas McK. Hughes, *The Life and Letters of the Reverend Adam Sedgwick*, 2 vols (Cambridge 1890), Vol. II, pp. 83–4.
11. [Adam Sedgwick] "Natural History of Creation", *Edinburgh Review* 82:1–85, 1845.
12. Adam Sedgwick *A Discourse on the Studies of the University of Cambridge*, the Fifth Edition, with Additions, and a Preliminary Dissertation (London, Parker 1850).
13. Adam Sedgwick, "Address to the Geological Society, 1831". *Proceedings of the Geological Society* 1:281–316, 1831, pp. 313–14.
14. William Buckland, *Vindiciae Geologicae: or, the Connection of Geology with Religion Explained* (Oxford 1820); *Reliquiae Diluvianae, or Observations on the Organic Remains Contained in Caves, Fissures, and Diluvial Gravel, and on Other Geological Phenomena attesting to the Action of a*

Universal Deluge (London, Murray 1823). See also, Milton, Millhauser, "The Scriptural Geologists, an Episode in the History of Opinion". *Osiris* 11:65–86, 1954.

15. William Cockburn, *The Bible Defended Against the British Association* (1844), 5th edn. (London, Whittaker 1845), p. 1. See also Francis C. Haber, *The Age of the World, Moses to Darwin* (Baltimore, Hopkins 1959).
16. Cockburn (1845), p. 24.
17. p. 42.
18. Charles Darwin, *On the Origin of Species by Means of Natural Selection, or the Preservation of Favoured Races in the Struggle for Life* (London, Murray 1859). Facsimile reprint (N.Y., Atheneum 1967), p. 488.
19. Leonard Huxley, *Life and Letters of Thomas Henry Huxley*, 2 vols. (London, Macmillan 1900), Vol. I, 179–89. Cf. *The Athenaeum*, 14 July 1860), pp. 64–5, and Donald Fleming, *John William Draper and the Religion of Science* (Philadelphia, Pennsylvania 1950), ch. 7 (The confrontation was occasioned by Draper's paper to Section D, "On the Intellectual Development of Europe, considered with Reference to the Views of Mr Darwin and others, that the Progression of Organisms is determined by Law", and Fleming provides a balanced account of the much-disputed encounter.)
20. [Samuel Wilberforce], "Darwin's *Origin of Species*", *Quarterly Review* 108: 225–64, 1860, p. 258.
21. Frederick Temple, *et al.*, *Essays and Reviews* (London, Parker 1860); [Frederic Harrison], "Neo-Christianity", *Westminster Review* 18:293–332, 1860; [Samuel Wilberforce], "*Essays and Reviews*", *Quarterly Review* 109:248–305, 1861; [A. P. Stanley], "*Essays and Reviews*", *Edinburgh Review* 113:461–500, 1861. Innumerable pamphlets appeared attacking the authors. Six volumes of them are collected in the Cambridge University Library.
22. John Tyndall, *Address Delivered before the British Association assembled at Belfast, with Additions* (London, Longmans, Green 1874), pp. 63–4; cf. "Apology for the Belfast Address" (1874) and "The Rev. James Martineau and the Belfast Address". Reprinted in John Tyndall, *Fragments of Science: a Series of Detached Essays, Addresses and Reviews*, 7th edn., 2 vols. (London, Longmans, Green 1889), Vol. II, ch's X and XI; Eve, A. S. and C. H. Creasey, *Life and Work of John Tyndall* (London, Macmillan 1945) ch. XV.
23. Cyril Bibby (ed.), *The Essence of T. H. Huxley: Selections from His Writings* (London, Macmillan 1967).
24. I am indebted to Fr Derek Holmes of St Edmund's House, Cambridge, who provided this example from his most interesting research on Newman.
25. Thomas H. Huxley, *Man's Place in Nature* (1863). Reprint (Ann Arbor, Michigan 1959), pp. 112–38.
26. William Whewell, *The Philosophy of the Inductive Sciences, Founded upon their History*, 2 vols. (London, Parker 1840), Vol. II, pp. 150 & 148. I am greatly indebted to Walter F. Cannon, whose interpretation of Darwin's work as an *expression* of natural theology has been a most important influence on my own rendering of the Darwinian debate. See "The Basis of Darwin's Achievement: a Revaluation", *Victorian Studies*, Dec. 1961, pp. 109–34.
27. Baden Powell, *The Connexion of Natural and Divine Truth: or, The Study of the Inductive Philosophy considered as Subservient to Theology* (London, Parker 1838); *Essays on the Spirit of the Inductive Philosophy, the Unity of Worlds, and the Philosophy of Creation* (London, Longman, Brown, Green, & Longmans 1855), Essay III; "On the Study of the Evidences of Christianity", Temple et al., *Essays and Reviews*, 1860, op. cit. (see above, note 21), p. 139. Cf. Powell, 1838, op. cit., pp. 268–9, 306–7. Powell, 1855, op. cit., p. 466, shows Powell's separation of man's moral nature from his physical constitution. For letters from Darwin to Powell, see Sir Gavin de Beer,

"Some Unpublished Letters of Charles Darwin", *Notes and Records of the Royal Society* 14:12–66, 1959, pp. 51–4. Darwin praises Powell's "Philosophy of Creation" in later editions of *On the Origin of Species*, 6th edn., 1872, p. xx. I am indebted to Professor Owen Chadwick for drawing my attention to the fact that Powell's works were read only by the intelligentsia. This was the germ of the interpretation of the debate in pp. 16–21 of this talk. See Owen Chadwick, *The Victorian Church, Part I* (London, Black 1966), ch. viii, sect. 3, especially pp. 553–6.

28. [Thomas D. Whitaker], "Gisbourne's Natural Theology", *Quarterly Review* 21:41–66, 1819.

29. William Cockburn, op. cit. (see above, note 15), "Appendix"; cf. Clark and Hughes, op. cit. (see above, note 10), Vol. II, pp. 76–80.

30. See above, note 20.

31. John W. Draper, *History of the Conflict between Religion and Science* (London, King 1875); Andrew D. White, *A History of the Warfare of Science with Theology in Christendom*, 2 vols. (1896) Reprint (N.Y. Dover 1960); James Y. Simpson, *Landmarks in the Struggle between Science and Religion* (London, Hodder & Stoughton 1925). See also David Lack, *Evolutionary Theory and Christian Belief: The Unresolved Conflict* (London, Methuen 1957). (Not all of these authors advocated a conflict: they reflected a prevailing conception in their writings, whatever their own views on the matter.)

32. Alvar Ellegård, *Darwin and the General Reader. The Reception of Darwin's Theory of Evolution in the British Periodical Press, 1859–1872* (Göteborg, Universitets Årsskrift 1958).

33. Sir Francis Bacon, *Of the Proficience and Advancement of Learning, Divine and Human* (1605) in *The Works of Lord Bacon*, 2 vols. (London, Bohn 1850), Vol. I, p. 4.

34. [W. H. Fitton], "Geology of the Deluge", *Edinburgh Review* 39:196–234, 1823, pp. 197–8, 230, 233–4; William Buckland, *Vindiciae Geologiciae*, 1820, op. cit. (see above, note 14), pp. 28–9; [Charles Lyell], "Scrope's *Geology of Central France*", *Quarterly Review* 36: 437–83, 1827, p. 483; Adam Sedgwick, *Discourse*, 5th edn., 1850, op. cit. (see above, note 12), p. clxxii; Darwin, 1859, op. cit. (see above, note 18), p. ii. For an excellent discussion of the debate on scientific explanation in this period, see Walter F. Cannon, "The Problem of Miracles in the 1830s", *Victorian Studies* 4:5–32, 1960.

35. Powell, 1838, op. cit. (see above, note 27), p. 231; cf., p. 240.

36. [Robert Chambers], *Explanations: A Sequel to "Vestiges of the Natural History of Creation"*, 2nd edn. (London, Churchill 1846), pp. 95, 154–5; cf. *Vestiges of Creation*, 12th edn. (Edinburgh, Chambers 1884), pp. 155–6.

37. Mrs Lyell (ed.), *Life, Letters, and Journals of Sir Charles Lyell, Bart.*, 2 vols. (London, Murray 1881), Vol. I, pp. 467–9; Charles Babbage, *The Ninth Bridgewater Treatise. A Fragment*, 2nd edn (London, Murray 1838) *passim* (Herschel's views are quoted in the Appendix; see especially pp. 225–7); *cf.* Walter F. Cannon, "The Impact of Uniformitarianism: two letters from John Herschel to Charles Lyell, 1836–1837", *Proceedings of the American Philosophical Society* 105:301–14, 1961. Alfred R. Wallace, *Darwinism: An Exposition of the Theory of Natural Selection with Some of Its Applications* (London, Macmillan 1889), pp. 477–8.

38. Darwin, 1859 op. cit. (see above, note 18), pp. 84, 488.

39. Charles Darwin, "Sketch of 1842", in Darwin and Wallace, *Evolution by Natural Selection* (Cambridge 1958), p. 86.

40. Herbert Spencer, *An Autobiography*, 2 vols. (London, Williams and Norgate 1904), Vol. II, p. 6.

41. A. P. Stanley, "The Religious Aspects of Geology (Funeral Sermon on Sir Charles Lyell)" (1875). Reprinted in A. O. J. Cockshut, (ed.), *Religious Controversies of the Nineteenth Century* (London, Methuen 1966), p. 250;

Francis Darwin, (ed.), *The Life and Letters of Charles Darwin*, 3rd ed., 3 vols. (London, Murray 1887), Vol. III, Appendix I; Amy Cruse, *The Victorians and Their Books* (London, Allen and Unwin 1935), p. 107.

42. Frederick Temple, *The Relations between Religion and Science* (London: Macmillan 1884), p. 188.

43. Anon. "Dr Lushington's Judgment", *Westminster Review* 22:301–15, 1862. *Cf.* Basil Willey, "Septem contra Christum", ch. IV of *More Nineteenth Century Studies* (London, Chatto & Windus 1956) and John Hunt, *Religious Thought in England in the Nineteenth Century* (London, Gibbings 1896), ch. XIV. When Temple was appointed to the bishopric of Exeter in 1869, a High Church journal described the event as "the darkest crime which had been perpetrated in the English Church" [Quoted in L. E. Elliott-Binns, *English Thought, 1860–1900: The Theological Aspect* (London, Longmans, Green 1956), p. 25].

44. Quoted in Henry F. Osborn, *From the Greeks to Darwin: An Outline of the Development of the Evolution Idea* (N.Y., Macmillan 1894), p. 141.

45. Lyell, 1827, op. cit. (see above, note 34), pp. 474–5.

46. Herbert Spencer, "Progress: Its Law and Cause", *Westminster Review* 11:445–85, 1857, p. 484. (The texts of this and other essays reprinted in Spencer's *Essays: Scientific, Political and Speculative*, 3 vols. (London, Williams and Norgate 1901) were considerably altered in the light of Spencer's later views.) Spencer had argued for inevitable progress before he had worked out his evolutionary theory. See *Social Statics* (London, Chapman 1851), p. 65.

47. pp. 484–5.

48. John Burrow, *Evolution and Society: A Study in Victorian Social Theory* (Cambridge 1966), pp. 98–9, 111, 222.

49. Darwin, 1859 op. cit. (see above, note 18), pp. 484–90.

50. Richard Hofstadter, *Social Darwinism in American Thought* (1944), revised edn. (Boston, Beacon 1955); Stow Persons, (ed.), *Social Darwinism; Selected Essays of William Graham Sumner* (Englewood Cliffs, New Jersey, Prentice-Hall 1963).

51. Walter Bagehot, *Physics and Politics, or Thoughts on the Application of the Principles of "Natural Selection" and "Inheritance" to Political Society* (1867), (London, King 1869). Cf. C. H. Driver, "Walter Bagehot and the Social Psychologists", in F. J. C. Hearnshaw, (ed.), *The Social and Political Ideas of Some Representative Thinkers of the Victorian Age* (1933) Reprint (London, Dawsons 1967), ch. IX.

52. Alfred R. Wallace, "The Development of Human Races under the Law of Natural Selection" (1864). Reprinted in *Natural Selection and Tropical Nature: Essays on Descriptive and Theoretical Biology* (London, Macmillan 1891), p. 185.

53. Alfred R. Wallace, op. cit., 1901 (see above, note 4) p. 380.

54. pp. 388–9. The verse is by J. H. Dell. I have been unable to obtain any information about him.

55. Ronald L. Meek, (ed.), *Marx and Engels on Malthus* (N.Y., International 1954), p. 171; cf. pp. 172–88 for selections from Marx and Engels on Darwin. Darwin held a very different view. He wrote, in 1879, "What a foolish idea seems to prevail in Germany on the connection between Socialism and Evolution through Natural Selection" [Francis Darwin, *The Life and Letters of Charles Darwin*, 3 vols. (London, Murray 1887), Vol. III, p. 237].

56. Sir Gavin de Beer, *Charles Darwin* (London, Nelson 1963), p. 266. Cf. Isaiah Berlin, *Karl Marx; His Life and Environment* 2nd edn. (London, Oxford 1960), p. 239, and Gertrude Himmelfarb, *Darwin and the Darwinian Revolution* (London, Chatto & Windus 1959), p. 316 and ch. XIX.

57. John W. Draper, *A History of the Intellectual Development of Europe.* (1861), 2 vols., (London, Bell 1909), Vol. I, p. iii. See also above, notes 19 and 31.

2

Evangelicalism and the Victorians

GEOFFREY BEST

Evangelicalism in the sense used here was a movement within the Protestant Christian world, beginning in the early eighteenth century and suffering no perceptible check to its development and diffusion until the middle or later years of the nineteenth century. It was a movement both of enormous psychological power in the lives of individuals and of great physical energy in its capacity to spread and circulate through all parts of society. Already by the early Victorian years much of British society seemed to be variously affected by this still flowing flood of ideas, ideals, and influences. As a "movement" it was quite unlike the Oxford Movement with which it is conventionally bracketed in the books as one of the two main religious forces forming the religious world of nineteenth-century Britain. It may indeed be a mistake on my part to use the word "movement" at all, because Evangelicalism and the Oxford Movement were totally dissimilar in origins, character, and effects. Evangelicalism was largely lay and often anticlerical in character while the Oxford Movement was essentially clerical and ecclesiastical. Evangelicalism was in some parts popular, even proletarian; its leadership was as socially varied as its rank and file; and its energies were entirely unpredictable. The Oxford Movement on the other hand was, in conception and leadership, *élitist*; more precise, more disciplined, and more institutional. For the social and political historian the Oxford Movement is of much less moment than Evangelicalism because, while the Oxford Movement's influence was clear and strong enough within the Anglican communion, Evangelicalism mattered enormously outside as well as inside the Church of England, and outside the religious world altogether. Historians of British society and culture in the nineteenth century all, I think, agree that Evangelicalism was in some ways responsible for some of its dominant characteristics. What we are not so sure about is exactly how far its influence reached and how it got there. Later on I shall look to see what relation there was between Evangelicalism and the Victorians, and produce a few suggestions as to where its influence may have been most substantial and undeniable. But to begin with I want to establish what the character of Evangelicalism as a religious movement was. Only after getting its origins and character clear can we dare to study its impact on the Victorians; and, since my (admittedly inexpert) eye detects less change than continuity in Evangelical thought and practice, analysis of its eighteenth-century origins will serve also as definition of its nineteenth-century character.

In its origins it seems to have been a reaction against certain features of the orthodox theology and religious outlook of the early Enlightenment. It was an attempt, so to speak, to supply the defects of that orthodox theology from the common man's point of view—a recovery, from the inherited arsenal of Protestant divinity, of certain doctrines and practices upon which Enlightenment and Catholic Christians, for very different reasons, laid no great stress. Evangelicalism stressed conversion rather than baptism as the important occasion of entry into Christ's Church. It stressed the scriptures rather than tradition or ecclesiastical authority as the source and test of religious truth. It stressed "The Word" working through preaching and prayer rather than sacerdotally administered sacraments as the main channel of grace. It stressed "Faith alone" as the Christian's means of salvation: salvation through Christ's atoning sacrifice, not through meritorious works or a mixture of faith and works. While by no means decrying good works, the Evangelical felt inspired and assured of his salvation because of his faith, and he regarded his works not as a claim for salvation but more as proof of salvation. Evangelicals put original sin right to the forefront of the religious mind, sometimes in the forbidding guise of "total depravity". Against the Enlightenment idea of God as a God of benevolent character who had made a world that was on the whole good and had put his creatures on their way to improving it to a still better state, Evangelicals asserted the idea of a God no less just and judicial than loving, whose justice demanded the capital penalty for all the fruit of that forbidden tree, and whose love and self-sacrifice alone opened a way of escape for faithful pilgrims. Evangelicalism brought the third person of the Trinity back into common circulation. The Holy Spirit had no prominent place in the cool and reasonable theology of the Enlightenment. Against its tendency to, so to speak, depersonalize God, to speak of God rather in such cold terms as the "Almighty", the "Supreme Being", the" Prime Mover", and so on, the Evangelical set the idea of God as intensely and immediately present, a Saviour directly and personally knowable, busy in and among his creation, intervening through acts of providence; the Holy Spirit hovering constantly over the Christian, answering prayer, still working miracles. God was felt to be watching so closely over every Christian that the Evangelical held it a prime duty to keep his every moment holy, safely answerable for at the Day of Judgment. Evangelicalism offered to release sinful man from the burden, the impossible burden as he viewed it, of earning his own salvation; the autobiographies of many early Evangelicals show how they were driven to embrace the Evangelical creed through what they discovered to be the impossibility of piling up enough "credits" to save them from the penalty of sin, the terror of the law. Evangelicals asserted that man could do nothing, either by works or by wishes for salvation, unless he was saved by Christ's freely offered grace. "Not the labours of my hands can fulfil thy law's demands. Could my tears for ever flow, Could my zeal no respite know, All for sin could not atone; Thou must save, and Thou alone." Evangelicalism offered to the layman more opportunity for active involvement in the work of his Church than did sacerdotalism (not that there was much of that in early eighteenth-century Britain) or ecclesiastical authoritarianism and ministerial monopoly. Chafing against the rules and regulations of an established Church rendered hypersensitive about free religious enterprise by a century of turmoil and a nasty experience at the hands of sectaries, the Evangelical called the saved to save others, to join in a common Christian work of rousing men to their spiritual danger and opening to them the gates of salvation. How could the saved not rejoice with others similarly saved? Why should they not associate to keep each other up to the mark, to make a community and fellowship of God's people? Evangelicalism wherever and whenever it was fresh, before it had become petrified and institutionalized, was a very social and co-operative thing.

These were the principal points of Evangelicalism as a religious mass movement. Of course so very extensive a "movement" was full of variety and change, and I am sure that experts will be able to say that in this or that respect I have exaggerated or falsified it. Historians of doctrine may fasten on to the Evangelicals' internecine debates on predestination and free will, and their undeniable tendency to slip towards antinomianism. These controversial elements were well recognized as such during the last third of the eighteenth century. But such controversial elements were much less significant than the agreed elements which characterized this (to use the Americans' term for it) "Great Awakening", and which marked each of the three main channels through which its lively impulses flowed towards the making of Victorian Britain.

One of these channels was Methodism: that part of the Evangelical phenomenon co-ordinated by George Whitefield and John Wesley, both of them Anglican clergymen increasingly neglectful of an establishment which increasingly neglected them. As that masterly organizer Wesley tirelessly toured the country he created in his wake and tied together through his pastoral care a nationwide connexion, the "united societies". In time it became known as the Wesleyan Connexion, though that was none of its founder's intention. This Connexion was a religious body with entirely its own ethos, essentially that of a laity sharing all the duties of a Church between them—evangelization and all the pastoral, administrative, and financial work of the Church; a nervous, striving, and joyful society, pushing on from "justification" to "sanctification"; a flexible, expansive, adventurous, and to begin with a very largely plebeian Church. Such was the first phase of Methodism, the phase which lasted until the death of John Wesley in 1791. During this phase its fissiparous proclivities were not notable. Before Wesley's death the only big secession was that of the Countess of Huntingdon's Calvinistic Methodist connexion, and with its theologian, Whitefield, Wesley himself had no difficulty in maintaining good relations; the agreed elements of Evangelicalism always being to him so much more important than the controverted ones. But after his death these fissiparous tendencies were uncontrolled and there followed a series of secessions from the main stem: first the New Connexion, then the Primitive Methodists, then the Bible Christians, then others. A principal cause of these secessions was the difficulty of defining the action of the Holy Spirit. Once it was admitted that special gifts might be poured by God into even the meanest and lowest of his faithful servants, it was difficult to deny that even the most unprepossessing and apparently unqualified Christian characters might be genuinely inspired by the Spirit; and if that inspiration took him out of a Methodist society it could also take followers with him. Thus these connexions often became known after the names of their virtual founders; the New

Connexion was called the Kilhamites, the Bible Christian the Bryanites; and so on. Another root cause of the secessions was the democratic and proletarian character of so much of the movement. Those who liked the atmosphere of a Methodist church as a religious democracy were bound to dislike the ministerial tendencies which developed after Wesley's death as his successors attempted to control the movement and to preserve its unity. The proletarian mind was prone to reject the hierarchical principle which asserted itself not only in ministerialism but also in the social differences which appeared within the movement as it increased its middle-class membership; and as each connexion grew, so the problems of order and cohesion mounted.

The second main channel through which the Evangelical impulse streamed towards the nineteenth century was the world of Nonconformity, *alias* (for our Victorian purposes) protestant Dissent. By this I mean that part of British Protestant Christianity which was neither within the established Church nor associated with John Wesley and the lesser Methodist organizers; i.e. "the three denominations" (the Presbyterians, the Independents, and the Baptists), the Quakers, and such obscure sects as the Muggletonians, the Sandemanians, and so on. Here was soil ready for the Evangelical sowing. Among these groups the memories of old puritanism had been kept alive and the Calvinist theology of puritanism retained. It was not surprising that Evangelicalism should find a warm welcome and an understanding public in the more ardently Trinitarian parts of Nonconformity—which generally meant the less intellectual parts, not moving towards Unitarianism. By the early nineteenth century it seems as if Evangelicalism had got into all the vital Trinitarian parts of Dissent. Only Dissent's Unitarian *élite*, drawing its dynamism and *élan* from quite different sources, was utterly untouched by it. Those parts of Dissent which had not gone Unitarian, if they had stayed religiously alive at all, were bound to have become more or less Evangelical. Indeed one sees the heart and soul of Evangelicalism nowhere more pungently expressed than by those pioneer Baptist missionaries who went to India in the 1790s and in those Congregationalists who pioneered "city missions" in the 1820s. (Were they an importation from New England, as Kay-Shuttleworth supposed?) The Baptists and the Congregationalists were the two dissenting denominations which were swelling fastest in numbers through the late eighteenth and early nineteenth centuries and from them most of the great leaders of Victorian Dissent would come: Edward Miall, R. W. Dale, Charles Spurgeon, John Clifford, *et hoc genus omne*.

The third main channel of Evangelicalism was the Anglican one. This channel of influence was perceptibly gouging its path through the religious terrain as early as the 1750s. Some time between then and the 1820s Anglicans started speaking about Anglican Evangelicals as "the Evangelicals", as if they were the only ones; and indeed, at the turn of the nineteenth century, they were the only ones who socially or politically mattered very much. But earlier in the eighteenth century this had not been the case and no sharp line divided "Anglican" from "non-Anglican" Evangelicals. The movement had appeared in every Protestant *milieu* and men were moved by it freely to cross and recross the formal boundaries between denominations. As numbers swelled and problems of organization became more acute, so members of the Established Church had increasingly to make up their minds whether they were going to stay within the Establishment and accept the limitations it set on their freedom of action, or whether they were to risk breaking its rules for the sake of the spiritual and missionary advantages which could only be gained outside its boundaries. John Wesley could not stay within the Established Church upon its own terms. He would not miss chances to preach the Word to souls that were dying around him. He pungently excused his disregard for the rules of the Establishment by asking men whether they thought that, when God asked him why he had not attempted to save such and such a one, God would accept the plea—"But, Lord, he was not of my parish." Plenty of Anglican ministers, however, did decide to stay in the Established Church, accepting its limitations and faults for the sake of its organizational advantages and whatever continuities of tradition and authority they believed it to hold from earlier Christian times. The second generation of Evangelical Anglican clergy worked within the Establishment, even setting up the claim which was peculiarly annoying to Bishops during the early nineteenth century—and was very difficult to deal with because there was so much truth in it—that they represented the central Anglican tradition established in the time of the Edwardian reformers.

So an Evangelical party appeared within the Church of England, as groups of like-minded clergy encouraged and supported each other in pockets all over the ecclesiastical map. Where these Evangelicals got together (and usually they came in clumps) they transformed Church life within their parishes and brought their parishes into social and religious communion with each other. They set a new model of an active parish clergyman—multiplying Sunday services, introducing week-day services and religious meetings in the evenings, founding societies for spiritual and charitable purposes, encouraging the laity to fill their non-working time with religious reading and activity, to do more and to venture more for their beliefs. All this was going strong before the 1780s, the decade which saw the second phase of establishment Evangelicalism inaugurated by the conversion of William Wilberforce and Hannah More, and the gathering around Wilberforce and his friends of the influential group known to history as the Clapham Sect. These men brought to Evangelicalism a social distinction and respectability it had not hitherto enjoyed. Under their banner the "Evangelical Party" became not (so far as one can measure) the most numerous, but certainly the most dynamic and ambitious element in the Established Church. By the 1820s it was in control of most of the great national religious societies and most local religious societies (which were probably more interdenominational than their national headquarters) were filled by adherents. It published and purchased the bulk of the popular Christian literature of the period: the Bible in all languages; classics of the Evangelical point of view from *The Pilgrim's Progress* to *The Dairyman's Daughter*; exegetical, homiletic, and soul-arousing works of every kind; and, in a more cultivated vein, those fine periodicals *The Christian Observer* and *The Eclectic Review*. It had perfected throughout the parishes that it controlled a richness and variety of parochial organization well designed to maintain an intense religious life among at any rate the sheep, and so to channel the charitable impulse as to promote at the same time religious and social discipline. By the accession of Queen Victoria, this Evangelical element within the Established Church was finely organized and articulated from London headquarters outwards to the provinces. Those headquarters lay in the offices of the great societies, gathered, most of them, in and around Exeter Hall, near the junction of the Strand and Waterloo Bridge. Its national leadership by the 1830s was consolidated among those bishops, peers, members of parliament, and metropolitan eminences of the ecclesiastical and business worlds who were to be found on the committees of all Evangelical societies. Its nationally organized societies linked its London headquarters with the humblest "auxiliaries" in the remotest parishes of the land and offered their delegates or representatives the annual excitement of the great May Meetings where notable orators treated their audiences every year to feasts of argument and flows of soul.

To sum up what I have said so far: Evangelicalism, unwittingly appropriated as a title by a party within the Established Church, demands that the social historian recognize it as a complex of religious attitudes and impulses, working through the hundred years preceding the accession of Victoria along three distinct channels of which Anglican Evangelicalism was only one. It so worked and spread through those hundred years that by the 1830s it was influencing very large numbers of people indeed. It had spread not only with the population explosion (as one would expect of any vigorous religious movement) but also through the successes of its evangelization. Its influence, moreover, touched many who were not themselves evangelically-minded and who might indeed not much like its theology; for example Sunday observance, the enforcement of the blasphemy laws, the encouragement of Sunday and day schools. And, finally, one sees it spreading as the central element of that moral revolution which was turning the fleshly, earthy, plain-spoken England of Fielding and Samuel Johnson into the conventionally respectable, carefully-worded England of Dickens and Matthew Arnold. (That summary contrast of course neglects *Pamela* at one end and *Jorrocks* at the other; but it is substantially true, none the less.)

This spreading, like most spreading, was, however, accomplished only at the cost of thinning, and such momentous diffusion was not achieved without some loss of rigour and concentration. One of our greatest historians of Victorian England, G. M. Young, speaks early in his famous *Portrait of an Age* of "the Evangelical discipline, secularized as respectability . . .". Another historian who has recently published a big, valuable, refreshingly controversial book about Anglican Evangelicalism, F. K. Brown, examines this process of diffusion and calls it "accommodation"; that is, making Evangelicalism palatable and manageable for the cultivated and gentlemanly classes, an attractive and exemplary model for the concurrence of piety and social position. One can argue about the extent to which that was a conscious aim for Wilberforce and his friends, and about the measure of their success, but that this was the tendency and effect of Evangelicalism during the revolutionary years seems to be undisputed. The moral revolution was accomplished. Frank sins of the flesh, along with much that was not so probably sinful, were driven into private or underworld or into lower-class life. The lineaments of Victorian respectability were well established by the time Victoria was learning the alphabet.

A few illustrations may stress the point. Sir Walter Scott's great-aunt, for example: a self-aware and intelligent old lady, renewing acquaintance in the 1820s with the novels of Mrs Aphra Behn, remarked how strange it was that she now blushed to look at books which, as a girl, she had heard read aloud to large family circles of God-fearing people. The Reverend John Bowdler, by no means a hard-line Evangelical, going through the works of Shakespeare and other classic authors, amended their immoral or dubious sentences to a harmless purity that could put no ideas into the simplest-minded maiden. Or compare pioneer with established Evangelicalism: Grimshaw of Haworth, fearless, indomitable, breaking up low sporting meetings and haranguing the crowds with such familiar warnings as "... And if you do perish, it shall be with the sound of the Gospel ringing in your lugs"; or John Wesley himself, badly beaten up and staggering out of Wednesbury where an attempt to spiritualize a wild community had gone wrong; compare them, I suggest, with the established "Evangelical pope", Dean Close of Cheltenham, influential, not unprosperous, preaching to the converted in a comfortable and rather luxurious church while the footmen waited for the owners of the fashionable carriages outside. My comparison seems no more unfair or risky than any historical impressionism has to be. I could certainly produce tough mob-quelling heroes in Dean Close's time, and self-sacrificing evangelists risking their persons in St Giles's and Bermondsey, in Gateshead, Chorlton-cum-Medlock, in Cornwall and Cannock Chase. But I could not find a Dean Close before the nineteenth century (unless it were the Countess of Huntingdon). That superior-class element simply was not in Evangelicalism until the time of Wilberforce, and fashionableness did not follow at once. Moreover, Evangelical zeal had by Victoria's time become somewhat deflected to foreign parts; deadlier Wednesburies, less deferential Haworths, were being tackled overseas; while that very roughness and violence which a Grimshaw had been able to control and a Wesley had sometimes suffered from was proportionately diminishing as the moral revolution and the improvement in the means of public order made at any rate the surface of British life less violent and brutal.

That ends my attempt to sum up the original character of Evangelicalism and what it had done for England by the 1830s. Now I turn to the Evangelical contribution to the "Victorian character" and to the character of Victorian England. One must begin with a few words about the so-called and much-written-about Evangelical Party in the Church of England through Victoria's reign and remark again that Evangelicalism in its proper sense is not the prerogative or the monopoly of a party of Anglicans. It is the more easy for non-professional historians, unless they are themselves Free Churchmen, to forget this, because so many of the books on the church history of modern England have been written by Anglicans who tend to equate "Church" with "Church of England" or "Catholic Church", and who pay not too much attention to such interesting facts as that about half the worshipping population was discovered in 1851 to be worshipping in non-established places of worship, and such interesting possibilities as that during the period 1860 to 1914, the proportion of worshippers in Established churches sank. So let us, while not neglecting Evangelicals in the Church of England, not forget that a greater number of Evangelically-inspired Christians must have been outside the Church of England.

Let us start then with the query: what were the relations between these two armies of presumed Evangelical allies? One must begin by admitting that their "official" relations were not too good, and that this was almost entirely because of the fact of Establishment. The Dissenters during the 1820s and 30s shifted from a general acceptance of the Establishment, as something neither wholly useless nor as disagreeable as it might be, to an attitude of general dislike, even detestation, of it. By the 1840s the Dissenters were fast coming to an agreement to destroy the Established churches if they could (they had all sorts of reasons for wishing to do this) and to reduce the Church of England to an equality of status with their own denominations, competing freely in an open market. Voluntarism was the official title of this view of Establishment and it was an attitude increasingly sympathized with by Methodists of every kind, by many Presbyterians, and by Irish Roman Catholics. And voluntarism had its political successes. For example it got rid of Church rates in 1868—it thwarted the Establishment assumption of sole responsibility for and control over national education—and it succeeded in disestablishing the Churches of Ireland (1869) and Wales (1914). This unhappy battle over Establishment raged from the early 1830s till the first World War, and during that period it intermittently absorbed the energies of most of the leaders of Church and Chapel (I am not so sure about local congregations) to the lamentable detriment of other matters where ground for co-operation and combination might more easily have been found. All this looks, from our further secularized standpoint, like a tragic irrelevancy, and yet a historian must present the issues as the Victorians met them in the Victorians' own terms. This dispute about Establishment caused a split among Evangelical Christians. Wilberforce and his friends had been censured by some of their stricter Establishment friends for con-

Alexander Melville

CHARLES HADDON SPURGEON

G. F. Watts

LORD SHAFTESBURY

Joseph Bonomi

DAVID LIVINGSTONE

sorting with Dissenters. The difficulty only got worse thereafter because Church of England Evangelicals, no matter how close their hearts and religious interests lay to those of Evangelical Dissenters, were after all deliberately staying within the Established Church and perhaps benefiting from the advantages of an Established Church about which the leaders of Dissenting opinion were from the 1840s using such language as "adulterous" and "drunk with the blood of saints".

Some high-placed Evangelicals, like that "Evangelical of Evangelicals" Lord Shaftesbury, never hesitated to co-operate with Dissenters of whom they approved, and a few well-known Anglican Evangelicals left the Church of England in the 1830s and 40s; the most celebrated of them, the Honourable and Reverend Baptist Noel, rejoiced to publicize his sympathy for what he believed to be the more apostolic state of denominational independence. But most Anglican Evangelicals would not let down the side of the Establishment and persisted in looking on Establishment as a condition more of advantages than nuisances. The nuisances they could, since the Established Church was such a libertarian and multi-coloured institution, usually ignore or circumvent; and it is instructive to see Anglican Evangelicals in the 30s and 40s flouting their bishops in the same way that the ritualists were to do later on, and getting away with it just as often. Among the principles of Anglican Evangelicalism in Victoria's reign one must therefore count the principle of Establishment.

But there was another principle not less dear to them, which was not so much a ground of division from non-Establishment Evangelicals as a ground of union with them: the principle of "No Popery". This affected their relations with outsiders in a very different way because feelings about Rome, ranging from cultivated distaste to deep and genuine horror, were shared by most of the Protestant public, and the Church of England Evangelicals, through their, so to speak, official position, helped give a lead to general Protestant thought which made them acceptably representative.

"No Popery", as part of a religious platform, inevitably lowered the tone of the movement which espoused it, and through "No Popery" there came into the Evangelical movement, especially in the persons of such as Mr Murphy, Father Achilli, and so on, a level of argument and a lowness of tone markedly different from what had been the case in Wilberforce's day. Perhaps some such difference was inevitable. Perhaps Wilberforce and his associates, working within the protection of a seemingly settled constitution and of conventions of gentlemanly politics, could afford to look more gentlemanly than their successors who were seeking both to lead and to represent in an age of perhaps coarse moral perception. Certainly post-Reform Bill politics were tougher and more publicly scrutinized than had been the case before the 1830s. The leaders of the religious public, like those of the political public, seem to have become increasingly conscious after 1830 of the demands of an anxious, periodical-fed, petition-signing public, with worries real or imaginary, about which that public wanted something done. Some such change in the character of relations between public men and public opinion may partially explain what happened to Evangelicalism about 1830. Not only did the leaders of the second great phase of the movement then die; Wilberforce, Hannah More, Charles Simeon, the last of Clapham's grandees, had all gone by 1836. Nor was it that the successors of the Clapham leaders were not men of the same personal stature—Shaftesbury and Fowell Buxton at any rate were not personally inferior to Wilberforce and Thornton—but Evangelicalism as a whole, including the Church of England part of it, seemed in the later 20s and early 30s to be shifting into a lower key. It is almost as if its greatest contribution had by then been made and as if it was felt to lack the breadth and tone of distinction which could satisfy many of its natural leaders in the post-revolutionary age—including, notoriously, so many of the sons of Clapham itself.

I conclude with a consideration of Evangelicalism's place in the history of Victorian society. Let us begin by considering some of the attributions usually made. First, with an eye on the disagreeable aspects of the case, I dispose quickly of "hell-fire". Evangelicals did not preach hell-fire any more than Roman Catholics or Tractarians. If there were more Evangelicals preaching hell-fire than there were Roman Catholics or Tractarians that was simply because there were more Evangelicals than there were Roman Catholics or Tractarians. Second, the alleged hypocrisy of the Victorians, often pinned peculiarly upon the Evangelicals: the preaching of double standards of morality or virtue, one for the prosperous, one for the poor; or one for public and one for private use; or the enforcement of a "morality" which was perhaps not "moral" at all. Of this charge it may at once be said that any society which keeps high ideals before its eyes is likely to fall below them; and for my part, as citizen and parent, I don't know whether I would prefer to live in a society professing high ideals and not coming up to them, or in a society become so suspicious and cynical about ideals that it is difficult for anyone with a persistent taste for them to indulge it. "Respectability" certainly did become an exigent standard—exigent enough to make social nonconformists at least uncomfortable—and in its prescriptions clear enough for anyone wanting to be thought respectable to know how to do so. There were all the conventions and taboos which, if properly observed, were a guarantee of acceptance as "respectable": conventions and taboos about dress, about the use of Sunday, about the organization of home life, the Bible placed (on the coffee-table?) in the living-room, the regular prayers; more or less severe and suspicious attitudes towards entertainments like cards, dances, music, the theatre; prudery and all its absurd compromises with the demands of day-to-day life.

I am not sure how much of all this sticks especially to Evangelicalism. In the first place, the roots of the moral revolution which produced these conventions and taboos of respectability were not all Evangelical: some of them for instance seem to lie in the development of bourgeois society through the seventeenth and eighteenth centuries, coincidental with Evangelicalism rather than caused by it. In the second place, one can find exactly the same aspects of "respectability" in mid- and later-Victorian England not only in circles where High Churchmanship had become the thing, but also in circles where no churchmanship of any kind was acceptable. But one part of the charge of hypocrisy does perhaps stick more to Evangelicals than to Christians of other persuasions. Evangelicals did talk much more about piety, did more eagerly make profession of their faith, did flaunt their familiarity with sacred persons and symbols more than non-Evangelical Christians. There was a kind of fatal loquacity about them which turned too easily into cant, as earlier critics and satirists of puritanism had well known. Stiggins and Chadband stand on the hypocritical wing of the army of saints who used a ready-made language to publicize their popular faith. The properly converted Evangelical being familiar with a personal Saviour, his language seemed, to many, embarrassingly intimate with sacred things, and fell often under the suspicion of not being entirely sincere. Thus G. B. Shaw, wishing to portray the subtlety with which the hypocritical could sponge upon the benevolence of the Salvation Army, made his Cockney loafer Snobby Price reply to Major Barbara's assistant, when she asked him if he had got a piece of bread, that he'd got the piece that mattered more, the peace that passed all understanding. Thus also the mid-Victorian clerical reviewer Conybeare found in the *Record* newspaper, the organ of strictest Evangelicalism, many absurd advertisements requiring Evangelical qualities even in "good plain cooks". But even when there was real sincerity and thought in the popular application of Evangelical language, it could offend and upset through seeming tasteless and demeaning to the sacred persons; "where prophets and apostles 'stood trembling', he is at his ease; where they adored, he declaims", as James Stephen wrote of George Whitefield. Or it could be mere mindless parroting, as it often was in Barbara Wilberforce's letters to her sons.

This charge of mindlessness brings us to the further allegation that Evangelicalism was unintellectual, even anti-intellectual. There is something in this too, though like all these charges it needs qualification. If it is meant that Evangelicalism was anti-scientific, then Evangelicals until at any rate the last quarter of the nineteeth century seem to me to have been in no different case from High Churchmen. This side of religious history is not one of my specialities, but I have detected no more intelligent an attitude among High Churchmen than among Evangelicals towards geology, for example, or towards Darwin and Darwinism, and at least one of the century's greatest scientists was Evangelical in his religious life—the incomparable Faraday. If the charge of anti-intellectualism is taken to mean that Evangelicals were uncritical and unintelligent about the holy Scriptures, then they again seem to have been in no different a case from many of their Christian contemporaries. Lord Shaftesbury, for one, with his cautious but none the less earnest interest in the prophecies and his alacrity to see the working of special providences, was surely neither more nor less "superstitious" than Newman with his credulity about the lives and works of "saints" and about miracle-working relics. Pusey in Tom Quad was no more "intelligent" about the Book of Daniel than Spurgeon in his tabernacle; the minds of both men were sealed to the workings of scientific biblical criticism; and, if we want any further proof of the essential harmony of Evangelical and High Church standards in these matters, we have only to witness the way in which the unreflective of both parties ganged up against *Essays and Reviews*, Colenso, and Jowett. But there is a difference about the Evangelical kind of anti-intellectualism. Evangelicals were, by comparison with High and Broad Churchmen, as the nineteenth century wore on increasingly cut off from the institutions and traditions which could have kept them in touch with intellectual and scientific progress. They were cut off because of their own party character. Evangelicalism never much valued worldly learning; in so far as international connections were concerned they had more in common with the fundamentalists of the United States than with any European group, while from the whole of the Roman Catholic world, its liberal and progressive as well as its ultramontane and reactionary parts, they were of course entirely shut off.

Evangelicals, moreover, were much more individualistic. There were few lines of principle to keep the ardent Evangelical from starting a society, a mission, or even a "church" on his own, whether he was Anglican or Dissenter or Methodist. He was free to do more or less whatever he liked. He was under no obligation to consult or obey a bishop. He might gain more friends than he lost if he incurred the censure of elders, trustees, synod, or conference. His was a world in which the Holy Spirit encouraged religious free enterprise, a world where (as a seemingly voluntarist writer in the *Contemporary Review*, 1869, observed of the founding nine years earlier of the Royal Navy Scripture Society) Evangelicals delighted to "show what freedom of action can effect in religious matters, unsupported and unblasted by secular authority". So there were sown broadcast the seeds of myriad separate institutions, schools, charities, colleges, chapels . . . : "Undenominational, but still the Church of God, He stood in his conventicle and ruled it with a rod." And all such Evangelical sprouts and offshoots quickly and easily became isolated from whatever branch of whatever main stem had been their origin. We may also note that Evangelicals were rather shut off from the high educational standards that were possible only for the *élite*. They were shut off by their spiritual egalitarianism. More scope was afforded to sheer ignorance by Evangelicalism than by any other major parts of the Christian world. Rich and poor being really equal in the eyes of God were equally likely, in Evangelical theory, to receive special gifts of the Holy Spirit.

Now we come to a side of Evangelicalism where its record is, I believe, more nearly impregnable: the field of social reform, the "humanitarianism" which is so often said to be a stamp of Victorian civilization, and which some Evangelicals took up very conspicuously, although others no less conspicuously kept out of it as smacking too much of this world. (Shaftesbury was not the only humanitarian Evangelical to complain that many of his own side let him down.) I have my eye especially on things like the anti-slave trade and anti-slavery movements, and the extraordinary record of an arch-philanthropist like the seventh Earl of Shaftesbury, to whom I see in Britain no High or Broad Church or Roman Catholic parallel. For that matter I can find no parallels to the whole team of major Evangelical philanthropists whom one could put alongside Shaftesbury, despite quite strenuous efforts to do so; the claim conventionally made by its party historians that Evangelicalism was responsible for virtually the whole of Victorian humanitarianism naturally stimulates one to contradiction. The issue is confused by a good deal of *odium politicum*, it having been a standard criticism of Establishment Evangelicals since Hazlitt's day that, however soft-hearted they were in social matters, they were politically very conservative, subtly serving conservative aims by diverting the attention of the "oppressed" from the radicalism and revolutionary activity which was their proper response.

Another charge levelled from Hazlitt's time onwards was that Evangelical humanitarianism was less effective than it might have been because it distracted attention and effort from domestic to overseas needs. I must leave the first as it is stated. It is certainly not true that Evangelicals (in my large sense) politically were all conservative during Victoria's reign, whatever they had been earlier on; but no doubt it is true that the effect of Evangelical social and charitable work, like most Christian social and charitable work financed and run "from above", must have tended to ally rather than to antagonize the classes.

The second charge, that there was a diversion of mission and money from domestic to overseas fields, surely has some truth in it. Evangelicals virtually invented modern missionary work. (The claim made by some anti-Evangelicals that the great step forward in missionary work was made much earlier by the S.P.G. seems to me absurd.) Enthusiasm for missions among the Evangelicals was huge and we may well wonder why. Partly, I suppose, because the missionary world was remote and romantic; partly because heathens who bowed down to wood and stone were rather more exciting than local lapsed Christians who were often dirty, drunken, and dangerous. Overseas missionary work was a kind of challenge more bearable, perhaps, to the educated mission-minded Evangelical than the contemporary equivalent of taking the road to Wigan pier. Moreover, the hastening of the Second Coming, which by some readings of Scripture had to wait until the Gospel was sounded among all nations, encouraged Evangelicals more than it encouraged others to undertake overseas missions among the pre-Christian heathen. Whatever the reasons, the result was the well-known one that Evangelical communities were passionately interested in missions; subscribed to them, read about them, listened to lectures and sermons about them, undertook missions themselves. Evangelical laymen were free to do more in the field of missionary work than High Churchmen. Perhaps more of this money and energy would have gone into domestic charities if so much had not been so powerfully attracted to overseas missions; or perhaps it wouldn't; I know no means of discovering. But of money and service for home needs there was an abundance and I think two important Evangelical distinctions may be seen; first, in the lengths to which their charitable work went, second, in the means by which they did it.

It seems to me that Evangelicalism did produce more enterprising and bold philanthropy than the other British brands of Christianity. This is the credit side of that free enterprise and religious individualism which stamped the Evangelical world and it might not have blossomed but for the Evangelical belief that miracles still happened. Of course many enterprises failed, or went awry. Shaftesbury's recurrent disappointment at the failure of enterprises begun under the most favourable auspices and backed by the most fervent prayer makes one quite sad at times that he had so little worldly wisdom. Evangelical saints were always being taken in by hypocritical rogues. But some of their great enterprises came off, and the volume of enterprise was very great. Consider Shaftesbury. Look at the list, at the back of Hodder's big biography, of the host of charitable institutions which sent representatives to his state funeral. Such tropical fecundity of institutions may have meant the complete waste of charitable resources that it certainly did to the tough organizers of the Charity Organization Society, but it can also be read as evidence of the enterprising adaptability of Evangelical charity, of its readiness to get into situations of particular need with appropriate particular remedies; and I think that that was rather distinctive. Consider also as evidence of this the life and work of the Reverend Andrew Reed, the influential Congregationalist who died in 1861. Although he engaged in many lesser lines of philanthropy, he had one special line which he pursued over forty years, and by the time he died he had got going such valuable institutions as the London Orphan Asylum, the Infant Orphan Asylum, the Asylum for Fatherless Children, the Asylum for Idiots, and the Royal Hospital for Incurables. The means by which he did this were fairly standard ones within the Evangelical community: the immense hard work of assembling backers and guarantors of funds, of publicizing, sermonizing, collecting subscriptions, using the ready-made Evangelical networks of societies, lecture tours, public occasions and so on, like a great philanthropic *entrepreneur* or operator, bringing together the capital, the administrative expertise, the voluntary help, which could create and leave to be absorbed into our Welfare State such great and essential institutions as those in which he specialized.

This big-scale, big-businesslike philanthropic operation, equally with that of the little local hand-made charities for the particular needs of particular communities, was I think a distinction of Evangelicalism: something Evangelicals did before anyone else, and more than anyone else. I don't think it is part of this distinction, as is sometimes claimed, that they alone took Christianity in among the working classes. It is possibly true (though it is more often asserted than demonstrated) that, as slum parsons of the Church of England, High Churchmen were more successful than Evangelicals. Ritualists were certainly more spectacular, but that is not the same thing; and party historians who write them up as if they were the only Christians who evangelized the slums forget all the non-Anglican Evangelicals who were at work long before the ritualists in the dark areas of British cities: the city missionaries who were busy from the 1820s onwards, lay evangelists (prototypes of the Establishment's "scripture readers"), the Unitarian and Congregationalist Domestic Missionaries, and so on; and in all this there was much originality and enterprise and an appropriate common touch.

I come in conclusion to an element in Evangelicalism which may have been especially important, and that is the way it dealt with Death. Evangelicalism indeed offered no more certain a conquest of it than did High Churchmen or Roman Catholics; but they did offer more homely and practical, and therefore more popular, techniques for handling it. I say "homely and practical" because they were within easy reach of the humblest, simplest, and youngest of Christians, and because families and friends could practise them at home on their own, without tarrying for any priest. Evangelicalism thus offered something of immense attractiveness and value. Pain and death and bereavement were for so many people for so much of the time facts of life which had to be familiarly faced up to and lived with. Death was not then the taboo which it has now become (almost by way of interchange with Sex). It was a confident and intelligible message that the Evangelical brought to the confronting of Death, and it was evidently of immense comfort to people who could never escape far from either, and who did not want or could not get the sacramentalist's alternative.

So that familiarity in the handling of holy mysteries which was so painful to cultivated Christians and refined agnostics was actually the heart of the Evangelical appeal and the essence of

Evangelical religion through the nineteenth as in the eighteenth century, and Evangelical literature and Evangelical diaries and biographies are full of death-bed scenes which may seem mawkish or sentimental or grotesque to our death-unaccustomed eyes, but which surely were very natural consequences of an efficacious facing of a great fact of life which demanded either a religious or a stoic answer. Death-bed scenes like those recounted in every monthly issue of the *Evangelical Magazine* mark the pages of all Evangelical literature, and what are we sophisticated moderns to make of it? In these descriptions of death-bed scenes there was of course much art; art certainly in the narrator, fashioning the incident to fit the model he had in mind; art perhaps also in the subjects of the stories, who knew well enough the model to which they were meant to approximate and who presumably took pains not to disappoint their loved ones by failing to produce it. (Witness Lord Shaftesbury's anxiety about the daughter who would not, for we know not what reason, produce in her quite serene death-bed the Evangelical formulae upon the expression of which he set such store.) There was evidently great comfort in this, the turning of the tables on death—"Death, thou shalt Die"—which was inexpressibly grateful to those who experienced it as well as those they left behind.

Death had no terrors for the Evangelical. I am not saying the Evangelical was thereby different from other sorts of believing Christian. I am suggesting that the Evangelical's confidence in the face of death was unusually comforting and homely; that it lay at the heart of Evangelical religion; and that it helps to explain both the boldness of Evangelical enterprise and the way, the sometimes maddening way, in which they set about those enterprises—the mixture of apparently admirable faith and goodness with an inaccessible and irrefutable self-assurance. Evangelicalism discounted the calculating reason of common mortality. General Gordon's life—his many charities, evangelistic work, and self-imposed martyrdom—was quite characteristic of the Evangelical mind at its most highly developed. One cannot but admire this strange pious military man. And yet one cannot but sympathize with those who had to deal with him; for example Evelyn Baring, British agent in Egypt, whose attempts to control General Gordon in the interests of sensible imperial administration led him to complain that "A man who habitually consults the prophet Isaiah when he is in a difficulty is not apt to obey the orders of anyone."

NOTE

I have made no attempt in this popular exposition to provide scholarly references, but I should feel quite dishonest were I not to admit my great debt to Britain's prime authorities in this field: Dr John Walsh of the University of Oxford, and the Reverend Dr John Kent of the University of Bristol; who will, however, probably disapprove of parts of what I have written.

3

The Church Militant Abroad: Victorian Missionaries

MAX WARREN

At the outset I want to consider this subject in its setting within the general title of this series of lectures—"The Victorian Crisis of Faith".

Our contemporary use of the word "crisis" almost always carries with it the idea of something ominous, a suggestion of disaster as being possible if not probable, a word compounded of fear and anxiety. This is emphatically not how I understand "the Victorian Crisis of Faith". In the *Shorter Oxford Dictionary* there are two other definitions of the word "crisis" which for me hold greater truth, and that not only in regard to the Faith of the Victorians.

One definition says simply "a turning point in progress". Another speaks of "a state of affairs in which decisive change for better or worse is imminent". The thought that a crisis may portend a change for the better is almost totally absent from contemporary usage.

To those two definitions from the dictionary I would add this illuminating suggestion from the Chinese language. In translating the word "crisis" the Chinese use two ideograms. One means "danger" and the other signifies "opportunity". "Danger-opportunity"—that seems to me a useful understanding of our word. And I would always want to lay the accent on the word "opportunity".

Those three definitions afford clues to the significance of the Missionary Movement of the nineteenth century for the general subject of these lectures, "The Victorian Crisis of Faith".

In what follows I confine myself strictly to the reign of Queen Victoria, 1837–1901. The roots of the Victorian age, and most certainly the roots of Victorian faith, go far back into history. The capacity of ideas formulated during Victoria's reign to survive her death and to influence politics and social living even today are sufficiently notorious to lead us to question whether we are not still in many respects Victorians. I am aware of all this in deliberately limiting myself to the reign of Queen Victoria, and my quotations will all be taken either from that period or as accurately reflecting it.

Those three definitions require some brief consideration.

A turning point in progress. The enormous turmoil which characterized so much of the ecclesiastical life of Britain during Victoria's reign tended towards introversion. The political and social struggle between the Established Church and dissent; the fears generated by what was known as the "Roman Mission"; the apparent life and death struggle between theology and science; the intractable nature of the problems posed by industrialism and the growth of cities; and an underlying fear of social and political revolution; all these combined to limit men's horizons, and to create an atmosphere which could be described as "The Victorian Crisis of Faith", using the word "crisis" after our contemporary fashion.

Now it was the missionary-minded members of all the Churches who steadfastly pursued a vision, which was literally world-encompassing, who can be seen today to have been those who proved that the crisis was a "turning point in progress".

A decisive change for better or for worse. As, in a small way, an historian of the Missionary Movement I am very well aware of the weaknesses and errors which have characterized missionary work. I have so many Asian and African friends, and have travelled so widely in those continents, that I think I am as conscious as anyone can be of the grounds upon which many Asians and Africans criticize the Christian missionary enterprise. Nevertheless I believe that the gains outweigh the loss and that the decisive changes to which missions have been a contributing factor have been for the better and not for the worse. If in no other way, then as pioneers of the truth that this is one world and that humanity is one, missions have been in the vanguard of the best thinking of modern times. The Victorian missionaries took a significant part in this pioneering.

Danger–Opportunity. In the reign of Queen Victoria the British Navy was busy charting the oceans of the world; explorers, for the most part British, were busy mapping the unknown; commerce somewhat tentatively was making use of the new maps. All this charting and mapping and commercial enterprise was dangerous. Modern medicine had not yet discovered the prophylactics which were to make life tolerable in the tropics. The death roll of all who ventured into these regions was prodigious.

In 1858 a party of six Roman Catholic missionaries landed in Sierra Leone. Within six months all had died of yellow fever. The Methodist Missionary Society and the Church Missionary Society, both from this country, could provide a comparable record as far as Sierra Leone is concerned. But the story is the same wherever you look. In a church in the heart of Peshawar City, hard by the entrance to the Khyber Pass, I have studied the monuments on the walls. One after another tells of young missionaries in their twenties who died of typhoid and dysentery.

But let an independent observer record his verdict on the way danger was accepted by missionaries and turned to opportunity. On 8 December 1896 Sir Harry Johnston, himself an explorer and colonial administrator with a vast experience of Africa, addressed the Ordinary General Meeting of the Royal Colonial Institute. In the course of his speech he said:

> The value of missionaries as pioneers of the civilization which this country seems impelled to extend in some instinctive race movement over the waste uncultivated tracts of the earth cannot be overestimated. These pioneers do not stop to ask whether it will pay to adventure their lives and their funds in these remote countries. They start on their self-imposed mission without *arrière pensée*; here they fail, there they succeed: if they die nobody takes much notice, and two men are always ready to supply one man's place. They make all the experiments and others reap the profit. On the results of their researches commerce is able to decide its timid steps, and eventually we possess sufficient data on which to determine whether it is right and necessary for the Government to seal with its intervention the work which these missionaries began.[1]

There are many comments which would today be prompted by that speech, and in particular the assumption of that notable empire-builder, Sir Harry Johnston, that running up the Union Jack was the seal on the good work done by the missionaries. The important point to note is the tribute that Sir Harry Johnston paid to the Victorian missionaries for their courageous determination to turn danger into opportunity. But if the dangers which they hazarded were dangers of death from disease, there is a deeper sense in which their interpretation of "crisis" went far to redeem the sordid record of religious bigotry and theological myopia which were enfeebling religious life in Victorian England and were tragically preparing the way for the retreat from religious faith which is so patent a feature of our own time. The Victorian missionary for all his limitations thought big and built largely.

I turn now to the subject allotted to me—"The Church Militant Abroad: Victorian Missionaries".

At the outset I would underline the adjective "Victorian". The missionaries we shall be considering were men and women of their own age. They shared with their contemporaries the basic assumptions upon which the prevailing temper of public life in Britain was based.

Earl Grey, Secretary of State for the Colonial Department in the administration of Lord John Russell (1847–52) could say in a book which he wrote in 1853:

> The authority of the British Crown is at this moment the most powerful instrument, under Providence, of maintaining peace and order in many extensive regions of the earth, and thereby assists in diffusing amongst millions of the human race, the blessings of Christianity and civilization.[2]

No Victorian missionary would have queried anything in that statement. It was an axiom he shared with virtually all his thinking contemporaries.

Two years later, in 1853, Gladstone, in one of his speeches, could say:

> It is because we feel convinced that our Constitution is a blessing to us, and will be a blessing to our posterity . . . that we are desirous of extending its influence, and that it should not be confined within the borders of this little island; but that if it please Providence to create openings for us in the broad fields of distant continents, we shall avail ourselves in reason and moderation of those openings to reproduce the copy of those laws and institutions, those habits and national characteristics, which have made England so famous as she is.[3]

The Victorian missionary would gladly say "Amen" to that. Before we laugh too loudly we might reflect on all the efforts made since World War II to provide each of the newly independent countries of the Commonwealth with precisely that Constitution which a hundred years ago Gladstone conceived to be the higher wisdom. Did Queen Victoria really die in 1901? I think she is still very much alive, though it is just possible that she is dying now.

So, as we look more closely at the Victorian missionaries let us remember that they were Victorians.

I divide my theme under three heads.

1. The Church Militant Abroad.
2. The Church Imperial Abroad.
3. The Church Prophetic Abroad.

1. THE CHURCH MILITANT ABROAD

I have already suggested that the Victorian missionaries had a view of the meaning of "crisis" which in the main distinguished them from the embattled religious enthusiasts in Britain. The most distinguishing characteristic was their profound conviction that the Christian gospel was not, in the first place, something to be argued about, but something to be proclaimed. And they took to themselves John Wesley's words "The world is my parish."

Who were these men? The evidence of the archives is quite clear that up until the 50s of the last century they were drawn from the ranks of "skilled mechanics". With rare exceptions the missionaries of the first half of the nineteenth century were, strictly speaking, "unlearned" men. Sydney Smith—that clever compound of malice and acidity whose wit enlivened the pages of the *Edinburgh Review*—was engaged at one stage in a quarrel with a man called Styles. Here is an illustration of Sydney Smith's controversal technique:

> Whoever wishes to rescue religion from the hands of didactic artizans —whoever prefers a respectable clergyman for his teacher to a delirious mechanic—whoever wishes to keep the intervals between Churches and lunatic asylums as wide as possible—all such men, in the estimation of Mr Styles, are nothing better than open or concealed enemies of Christ.[4]

Sydney Smith was firmly of the opinion that missionaries were "didactic artizans" and "delirious mechanics". So he could denounce the missionaries as those who would

> deliberately, piously, and conscientiously expose our whole Eastern empire to destruction for the sake of converting half-a-dozen Brahmins, who after stuffing themselves with rum and rice and borrowing money from the missionaries would run away and cover the Gospel and its professors with every species of impious ridicule and abuse.[5]

These words were written before Queen Victoria came to the throne and therefore, strictly speaking, fall outside our period. But two things are to be noted. Sydney Smith's malicious wit certainly helped to create in the public mind a stereotype of the missionary which lingered on right through the nineteenth century and well into the twentieth. No doubt, though more elegantly expressed, it is to be discovered in some quarters still.

The more important point to remember is that men whom Sydney Smith dismissed as "didactic artizans" and "delirious mechanics" provided the main source from which missionaries were drawn well into Victoria's reign. Until the second half of the century not many "respectable clergymen" joined their ranks: not many men with university degrees; but what they lacked of the more polished forms of learning they made up by hard work, devotion, and complete dedication to their task. A modern historian, L. H. Gann, has described such men in the Victorian age as "inner-directed men who got their education the hard way".[6]

Pause for a moment over that description. "Inner-directed men"—those words signify the driving force of spiritual conviction. Such men have formed the shock troops of the Church Militant under many forms. Members of the Jesuit Order have been such. So have Franciscans and Dominicans. Such men formed the hard core of Cromwell's "praying regiments". Ronald Knox's great study, under the title *Enthusiasm*, shows how widely dispersed they have been in the story of the Christian Church. The term "militants" describes them well.

And these missionaries, so fiercely pilloried by Sydney Smith, did in very many cases "get their education the hard way". I give you just one illustration out of the many I could quote. A young man, Thomas Norton, a cobbler, offered for service with the Church Missionary Society. One of his referees wrote of him in the following terms, recommending him for missionary service as

> a man remarkable for piety and application to learning, having an earnest desire to be a missionary, and warmly attached to the doctrine and discipline of the Church of England. In the course of a twelve months, by eating Greek and meals together in the interests of his trade, he had got some way on in his Greek Testament.[7]

He served in Travancore for twenty-five years and died early in Queen Victoria's reign.

A recent historian, Dr Gunson, in a very penetrating discussion of the missionaries we are considering, writes:

> Most of the Missionaries . . . whatever their experience or training, took with them into the field the New Mechanic's consciousness of his social position, his desire to better himself, and his dependence on, and obligation to, the less "fortunate".[8]

That sentence affords a clue to the achievements of those "skilled artizans". Part of their militancy was an expression of their own struggle to escape out of the ranks of the proletariat, the submerged mass of the labouring poor of the Industrial Revolution. To escape from that background you had to be a fighter. A social militant and a religious militant have much in common.

But militancy can take a variety of forms. An overwhelming conviction of the rightness of your cause and an insistance that your religion ought to be related to every aspect of life was a very common feature of these missionaries. In the year 1837, the year of Queen Victoria's accession, a missionary of the London Missionary Society, John Williams, published a book with the title *A Narrative of Missionary Enterprises in the South Sea Islands.*[9] In this book he described the natural history of the islands, the origin, languages, traditions, and usages of the inhabitants. The book soon became a bestseller. It is characteristic of the author and of his age that he then proceeded to address an "Appeal to the Merchants and Ship Owners of London". In this Appeal he made proposal

> for an extensive exploratory voyage for the purpose of extending the blessings of Christianity and civilization to the numerous islands and groups in the vast Pacific Ocean.[9]

He went on to make points calculated to appeal to businessmen:

> That the commerce of our country is materially benefited is evident by the fact that, at the lowest computation, a hundred and fifty or two hundred thousand persons, who a few years ago were unclothed savages, are now wearing and using articles of British manufacture: the cultivation of indigo, cotton, coffee, sugar, arrowroot, coconut oil, etc., have been introduced, and it is confidently expected that in a few years the islands now under Christian instruction will be of considerable commercial importance.[10]

Something of the same comprehensive outlook can be seen in the person of a missionary of the Church of Scotland, Hope Waddell. Horrified by the evidence of human sacrifices in West Africa a small company of missionaries and traders had formed a Society for the Suppressing of Human Sacrifices. Hope Waddell in 1849 got them to enlarge its objective and the Society was re-named The Society for the Abolition of Inhuman and Superstitious Customs and for Promoting Civilization in Calabar. Her Britannic Majesty's Consul, John Beacroft, joined the Society. It is an intriguing fact that the local African chiefs were told that if they had any difficulties about enforcing the reforms proposed by the Society, he would bring warships to their aid. We should note that

> these reforms included not only prohibitions of human sacrifice, twin-murder, and trial by ordeal, but also provision for such things as the right of the mission house to be an asylum, the Presbyterian conception of Sunday Observance, and Victorian dress fashions.[11]

Members of the Victorian Society will note that last point with especial satisfaction!

But I would not have you imagine that in the Victorian Age only professional missionaries represented the Church Militant. Anyone at all familiar with the story of the British role in India in Victoria's reign will know something of the profound and penetrating influence of the Evangelical movement in Britain upon both civilian and army officers. In particular a considerable argument developed as to the causes of the Indian Mutiny. It was widely reported that the Mutiny was provoked by a fear that the British Government was planning to force Christianity upon the population. Lord Ellenborough, for instance, the last President of the Board of Control of the East India Company, argued forcefully that Christian education accounted for "the almost unanimous mutiny in the Bengal army". This was widely publicized. A more judicious observer, Martin Richard Gubbins of the Bengal Civil Service, who was financial commissioner for Oudh, after a careful assessment of the various causes which lay behind the Mutiny adds this intriguing information:

> Nor do I think that of late years our missionary zeal in India has been tempered by wisdom . . . public official influence exercised in aid of missions has been too much felt . . . native gentry have been solicited by English civilians to subscribe to the Religious Tract Society; and . . . British colonels have preached the Gospel to their native soldiers in the public bazaars.[12]

In the reign of Queen Victoria the Church Militant Abroad took many different forms.

2. THE CHURCH IMPERIAL ABROAD

Reference will have been noted to British consuls in West Africa and British colonels in India. Those references form the link between the first and second divisions of my subject. I would now invite consideration of what I have called "The Church Imperial". I do not think that that is wholly a misnomer of the Church Militant Abroad in the latter part of Queen Victoria's reign.

I introduce what follows from an unexpected source, J. H. Newman. In the year 1852 he gave a notable course of lectures with the title "The Idea of a University". I quote from this because these lectures have had an enduring influence and Newman was certainly one of the ablest minds of that great century.

Having referred to the various associations and societies in which the human race has been organized Newman continues:

> But there is one remarkable association which attracts the attention of the philosophers . . . its bond is a common civilization, and though there are other civilizations in the world, as there are other societies, yet this civilization, together with the society which is its creation and its home, is so distinctive and luminous in its character, so imperial in its extent, so imposing in its duration, and so utterly without rival on the face of the earth, that the association may fitly assume to itself the title of "human society" and its civilization the abstract term "civilization".

After briefly acknowledging the existence of China, India, and the Arab world, Newman continues by saying that Western civilization

> has a claim to be considered as the representative society and civilization of the human race, as its perfect result and limit, in fact . . . I call then this commonwealth pre-eminently and emphatically human society, and its intellect the human mind, and its decisions the sense of mankind and its disciplined and cultured state civilization in the abstract, and the territory in which it lies *orbis terrarum*, or the World.[13]

In that passage there is vividly and forcefully expressed the fundamental assumption upon which Britain, in particular, justified its "dominion over palm and pine". In magnificent prose, wonderfully unaware of its astonishing presumption, you have a perfect expression of the Victorian mind.

Earlier I quoted from Earl Grey, one-time Secretary of the Colonial Department in Lord John Russell's administration, as holding that it was Britain's privilege to diffuse among mankind the blessings of Christianity and civilization. That was early in Queen Victoria's reign.

At almost the same moment as Newman was giving his lectures on "The Idea of a University", David Livingstone was writing to one of his subordinates in the Zambezi Expedition of 1858–63 with regard to the Africans they would meet:

> We come among them as members of a superior race and servants of a Government that desires to elevate the more degraded portions of the human family. We are adherents of a benign holy religion and may by consistent conduct and wise, patient efforts, become the harbingers of peace to a hitherto distracted and trodden down race.[14]

To quote that passage is not, in any way, to impugn the greatness of one of the greatest of the Victorians. I quote it only to illustrate something which I must describe as the imperial mind of the Victorian missionary in the second half of the nineteenth century.

Readers of Margery Perham's life of Lord Lugard will remember how Lugard, as a schoolboy in 1876, wrote an essay on courage in which he took as his illustration David Livingstone, and ended with the words:

> Justly we may regard him as a pattern of British courage and we shall not disparage England's other heroes by selecting him as the greatest among them.[15]

It is difficult not to believe that this estimate of his hero influenced Lugard's own devotion to his imperial mission.

Writing to a friend in 1902, Lady Lugard gives this picture of her husband:

> Sir Frederick has nearly killed himself—and I think a fair percentage of his staff too—with overwork. Yet they like it. After all they are working for an idea, and that is more than all men can say.[16]

The Church Imperial, like the Church Militant, when it found itself abroad took many forms. Nor is it properly a subject for surprise that missionaries (who were, after all, children of their age) absorbed and expressed in their own attitudes, as they did, those assumptions which Newman had so eloquently expressed. Nor can it astonish us if missionaries found it easy to accept the patronage of governments, as they did, seeing that so often the representatives of government, for one reason or another, offered that patronage. In a notable speech in the Albert Hall in 1895 Lord Rosebery in reply to a question "What is Liberal Imperialism?" is on record as replying:

> Liberal imperialism implies, first, the maintenance of the Empire; secondly, the opening of new areas for our surplus population; thirdly, the suppression of the slave-trade, fourthly, the development of missionary enterprise, and fifthly, the development of our commerce, which so often needs it.[17]

That reference to the suppression of the slave-trade is a reminder that all through the nineteenth century missionaries shared with other philanthropists in seeking by every means to keep the issue of the slave-trade before the eyes of the public.

I will bring this section to a close with a nice glimpse of that great empire-builder, Sir Harry Johnston. It is the year 1900. He is in Uganda. During a visit to the Basoga people he spoke through a missionary interpreter as follows:

> Tell them how interested the Queen is in their welfare, how she wants them to improve themselves and their country. We were like you long years ago, going about naked . . . with our war-paint on, but when we learnt Christianity from the Romans we changed to become great. We want you to learn Christianity and follow our steps and you too will be great.[18]

3. THE CHURCH PROPHETIC

In so interpreting my subject I have been attempting to present you with a candid picture of the Church Militant abroad and, in considering the Church Imperial, to show you the attitude of mind which, with a few rare exceptions, united missionaries, traders, and government administrators during the greater part of the reign of the "Great White Queen".

But this is not the whole story. While missionaries, traders, and government officials shared certain basic assumptions about the relationship of Christianity with western civilization and perhaps particularly the Victorian way of life, there was another dimension to the missionary of this period.

I would describe this under the title of "The Church Prophetic". By "prophetic" I mean the capacity to take long views and build for a distant future. Again I would safeguard myself from misunderstanding by insisting that "The Church Prophetic" was not confined to missionaries. Once again government officers, soldiers, and traders had their place, a very honoured place in this aspect of the Church Militant abroad.

Thomas Babington Macaulay in his famous speech on Indian Education in 1835 established the pattern of higher education in India through the medium of English. This determined the whole course of Indian education not only in the nineteenth century, but down to our own day. Indeed, the language riots in India during 1968 can be said to be in some measure a belated protest against this very policy. I was staying in a university town in North India during the height of the agitation at the end of 1968 and can testify to the force of Indian feeling in that part of India. Had the university students known a little more history they would have been better advised to burn an effigy of Macaulay than to waste their energies in ordering shopkeepers to cover up all English language signs and generally disrupt the whole life of the community.

Macaulay had been for a short time in India and had there

gained some knowledge of the educational enterprise of a Scots missionary, Alexander Duff. Duff was one of the pioneers of modern education in India. He had no narrow vision of the content of education and he combined wide views as to what constitutes a liberal education with a perspective which reached far into the future. Speaking in Scotland, while on leave in 1840, he defined his educational strategy:

> Spurning the notion of a present day's success, and a present year's wonder, we directed our view not merely to the present but to future generations.[19]

In that respect Duff and Macaulay had a prophetic touch about their policies.

A little over one hundred years later the British Government appointed a commission to investigate higher education in West Africa. Its chairman was the Right Hon. Walter Elliot. The report which was published in 1945 contained the following paragraph:

> When one looks for the root from which West African education sprang one comes back, everywhere and always, to the missionaries. It was the Christian missions who first came out to the coast without desire for fee or reward. It was the congregations in Britain and America who provided the first development funds, the pennies of poor people, expended without reckoning of capital or interest. . . . It was, and still is, the Churches who have made it possible to talk of West African education, higher, middle, or lower, as a fact and not merely as an ideal.[20]

There, I submit, is an interesting testimony to the Church Prophetic from an independent source. As impressive in its own way is this quotation from an article by Sir Harry Johnston written in 1912 but referring to the 90s of the last century. Something of his outspoken character burns its way through these sentences:

> The idea that there would ever be any serious demand on the part of the colonial peoples for a voice in their own taxation and government scarcely disturbed the forecast of any average imperialist . . . but, unfortunately for the ideals of the imperialist Britain of twenty years ago, education was permeating the British Empire in all directions . . . Missionary Societies were everywhere founding schools, colleges, and universities, attempting to make black, brown, and yellow people think and act like white Christians . . . impressing on them over and over again that once they were Christians and civilized, or even civilized without being Christians, they were the equal of any man, no matter of what colour or race.[21]

That is an intriguing testimony to the Church Prophetic. In this matter of education, the missionaries were looking a long way ahead. The present University of Sierra Leone began as a secondary school founded by a Missionary Society in 1829. At the same time they were doing something of vast cultural and psychological significance in the present moment of their efforts. A modern historian, P. Bohannan, himself no great sympathizer with the work of missionaries, writes thus:

> It is impossible to over-emphasize the influence that missionaries, particularly Christian missionaries, have had in Africa. . . . The great debt that Africa owes to missionaries is that in a situation in which the forces of trade, colonial government, and the missions themselves were creating cultural havoc, it was only the missions that began to rebuild, and gave them a chance to rebuild.[22]

A Chinese friend of mine once told me that the ideogram by which Chinese convey the idea of our word "telescope" is to call it "the eye that sees far". It is in their capacity to take long views that the Victorian missionaries most notably expressed the reality of the Church Prophetic. They had eyes that could see far.

But I sometimes think that the most dramatic of all missionary achievements was one that was never made deliberately. I refer to the phenomenal courage of, and the unique contribution made by, countless single women missionaries. They began to go to Asia and Africa in the second half of the nineteenth century. Their very presence helped to achieve three results. They demonstrated that there was another career open to women besides marriage. They raised the age of marriage. And they introduced the teaching and nursing professions as channels through which young Asian and African women could serve their own people.

The revolution thus achieved may yet come to be recognized as the most remarkable of all the remarkable initiatives for which the Victorian age was responsible.

The subject allotted to me was far too vast and complex to be satisfactorily dealt with in a single lecture. But having given my own interpretation of the general title of these lectures, "The Victorian Crisis of Faith", I hope that I have been able to demonstrate in some small way that it was the Victorian missionaries who in signal fashion made the Victorian Crisis of Faith into a "turning point in progress" by channelling religious devotion away from sectarian squabbling in England to a constructive Mission to the World: who ensured that the Victorian Crisis of Faith should be made to yield "a decisive change for better or worse" all over the world: who, in the best Victorian tradition looked at danger and discovered in it opportunity.

NOTES

1. *Report of Proceedings of the Royal Colonial Institute*, Vol. xxviii, 1896–7, p. 51.
2. Earl Grey, *The Colonial Policy of Lord John Russell's Administration* (London, Richard Bentley 1853), Vol. I, pp. 13–14.
3. Paul Knaplund, *Gladstone and Britain's Imperial Policy* (Allen & Unwin 1927), p. 203.
4. Sydney Smith, *Edinburgh Review*, April 1808, p. 143.
5. Sydney Smith, *Edinburgh Review*, April 1808, p. 119.
6. L. H. Gann, *A History of Northern Rhodesia—Early Days to 1953* (Chatto & Windus 1964), p. 38.
7. Charles Hole, *The Early History of the Church Missionary Society* (C.M.S. 1896), p. 125.
8. W. N. Gunson, *Evangelical Missionaries in the South Seas, 1797–1860* (Ph.D. Thesis for Canberra University. Unpublished. Typescript in L.M.S. Archives), pp. 33–4.
9. John Williams, op. cit. (London, J. Snow 1837).
10. Ebenezer Prout, *Life of the Rev. J. Williams* (London, John Snow 1843), p. 505.
11. J. F. A. Ajayi, *Christian Missions in Nigeria, 1841–1891—the Making of a New Elite* (Longmans 1965), p. 65.
12. Martin Richard Gubbins, *An Account of the Mutinies in Oudh and of the Siege of the Lucknow Residency* (Richard Bentley 1858), pp. 89–90.
13. J. H. Newman, *The Idea of a University* (edn. of 1959), pp. 248–51.
14. J. P. R. Wallis, ed., *The Zambezi Expedition of David Livingstone, 1858–1863* (London, Chatto & Windus 1956), Vol. II, p. 416.
15. Margery Perham, *Lugard—The Years of Adventure 1858–1898* (Collins 1956), p. 34.
16. Margery Perham, *Lugard—The Years of Authority, 1898–1945* (Collins 1960), p. 81.
17. T. F. Coates, *Lord Rosebery* (London, Hutchinson 1900), Vol. II, p. 789.
18. Roland Oliver, *Sir Harry Johnston and the Scramble for Africa* (Chatto & Windus 1957), p. 297.
19. George Smith, *Alexander Duff* (Hodder & Stoughton 1879), Vol. I, p. 108.
20. Report Cmd 6655 (London, H.M. Stationery Office 1945), p. 16.
21. H. H. Johnston, *Views and Reviews*, pp. 232–4.
22. P. Bohannan, *African Outline* (English edition, 1966), pp. 215–16.

4

Newman and the Oxford Movement

DAVID NEWSOME

The general title of this series of lectures is "The Victorian Crisis of Faith", and of all the subjects chosen perhaps this one on "Newman and the Oxford Movement" and Dr R. M. Young's opening lecture on "The Impact of Darwin on Conventional Belief" are the two which most obviously relate to the central theme. The Oxford Movement was a response to a sense of crisis.

"The Church in danger" was its slogan. Horror of revolution over the water (the barricades were up again in Paris in 1830 and a French King set off disconsolately on his travels), fear of revolutionary elements at home seduced into secularist conceits by the infamy of Tom Paine or the pretentious assumptions of the devotees of "Useful Knowledge", consciousness of change with the coming of railways bringing with it the acceleration of society towards its doom, dismay at the dissolution of the Tory Party over Catholic Emancipation and the rise of the Whigs to power, pledged to reform and prepared without scruple to ally with the forces of anti-clericalism in order to get their way—such were the tensions which drew churchmen of different traditions together, inspiring especially the younger and more fiery spirits amongst them to militant action, in a sure belief that a back-to-the-wall engagement would mark the "Thermopylae where the only effective stand should be made against the last inundations of lawless power".[1]

In March 1829, John Henry Newman wrote to his mother from Oxford:

> We live in a novel era—one in which there is an advance towards universal education. Men have hitherto depended on others and especially on the clergy for religious truth: now each man attempts to

> judge for himself. . . . All parties seem to acknowledge that the stream of opinion is setting against the Church.[2]

The sense of crisis gripped Oxford as it touched nowhere else. It was not only that Oxford was the traditional bastion of orthodoxy (that indeed would be a thesis not too easy to sustain for this period without innumerable qualifications), or that, being the home of lost causes, it was likely to react dramatically to the threat of the imminent demise of the Church of England. More pertinent is the fact that Oxford during the late 1820s and early 1830s boasted amongst its senior members a number of energetic and unusually talented young men who all had these three attributes in common: an ardent pietism, derived on the whole from an Evangelical upbringing, an incomparable training in logic acquired through leading the field in the most formidably competitive test which the English academic world could offer, and finally a growing veneration for the teaching and example of John Keble. Furthermore the furore over Catholic Emancipation in 1829 raged more vigorously and viciously in Oxford than anywhere else, and for good reason. Peel committed a *volte face* and divided the Tory party; and Peel was member for Oxford University. This was the issue which divided Oxford into rival parties and set the stage for the theological contests of the next decade.

For the next fifteen years Oxford was plunged into turmoil. Hardly for a moment did the sense of crisis relax. Mark Pattison, looking back on it all many years later, called it a nightmare.[3] Dean Church likened the atmosphere of this closely-knit and inward-looking University town to the storms which gripped the city-states of late medieval Italy—neighbour turning against neighbour, love and hate running to extreme.[4] Teachers and preachers whose disposition had marked them for a quiet life were thrust by a curious fortune into the role of party leaders, saluted as heroes or anathematized as blackguards, compelled to take sides on every political and theological issue of the hour. There was a universal consciousness of conflict and challenge, provoking great gestures and petty strife. We can sense the thrill of going into battle, when the first contributors to the *Tracts for the Times* marshalled their supporters and sent them riding off at break of day, satchels stuffed with tracts, to exhort the country clergy to magnify their office and to choose their side;[5] we can feel the tension in the Adam de Brome chapel of St Mary's, Oxford, as Newman unfolded in weekly instalments his *rationale* of the Anglican *via media*, his audience hanging on every word. Even the comic and the grotesque make a sort of sense in the heightened drama of these times: a Regius Professor deprived of his right to vote for select preachers because he had written a supposedly heretical book which few had read and nobody could understand;[6] dignified Heads of Houses and Doctors of Divinity hiding behind hedgerows to detect unwarrantable goings-on at Newman's supposed monastery at Littlemore;[7] and an eminent Headmaster of Rugby School slandered mercilessly because he had shown sympathy to dissenters and had allowed his pupils to discover that he had an eccentric and unconventional penchant for mixed bathing.[8]

What was it all about? It is a matter of some doubt whether the principals themselves would have been able to give the same reply to that question. The answer hallowed by convention is that supplied by William Palmer, writing of the clamour for reform and the anti-clericalism of 1833.

> We knew not to what quarter to look for support. A Prelacy threatened, and apparently intimidated; a Government making its powers subservient to agitators who avowedly sought the destruction of the Church. The state so long the guardian of that Church now becoming its enemy and its tyrant. Enemies within the Church seeking the subversion of its essential characteristics and what was worst of all—*no principle in the public mind to which we could appeal.*[9]

In short, the enemies were Erastianism, in the sense of the claim by the State to dominate the Church, and latitudinarianism, by which was chiefly meant the weak churchmanship and liberal principles of Thomas Arnold. From the negative point of view, then, the Oxford cause was not a High Church attack upon the Evangelicals—why should it be? This was the religious tradition in which Newman himself had been nurtured and with him many of the principal adherents of Tractarianism. The pietistic element in Pusey was intensely strong, even if he was critical of Evangelical attitudes and acknowledged no such party affiliation. The Evangelicals themselves were at one with the Tractarians in their opposition to Arnoldianism and Erastianism, and—because of the tensions within the party during the 1820s especially on matters of Church order and religious decorum—were, in the persons of the *sanior et valentior pars* at least, appreciative of the early efforts of the Oxford party to exalt the Church and defend ecclesiastical principles.[10]

It was not to be so for long, of course. And perhaps the sense of kinship was never more than superficial. The contrast is more clearly discerned when one turns to the positive aspects of the Oxford

Movement. The clue to this is supplied by Henry Edward Manning in a letter written to Edward Coleridge in October 1845, shortly after the sad news of Newman's secession to Rome, although long anticipated, had been confirmed. Did this mean that the Movement had been a failure? Was all their work undone? No, answered Manning. The state of the Church, the changed atmosphere, the new consciousness of what a Church should be and of the truths to which that Church must bear witness, prove it not so. "It is almost incredible," he wrote, "that a body which fifteen years ago was elated at being an Establishment should now be conscious of being a Church."[11] It was in the definition and elaboration of this ecclesiology, and the theological implications which followed therefrom—the exalted nature of the episcopate, the high sacramentalism, and especially the teaching on the nature of baptismal regeneration and the relationship of justification to sanctification—that the Evangelicals found themselves forced to part company from those who had seemed to be allies. And had they known more about the teaching of John Keble and the extent to which Keble had influenced Newman, they might well have drawn back from any expression of support from the beginning. This, however, requires some deeper reflection: in particular, a consideration of the respective attitudes of Newman and Keble, and an analysis of how these differences were reflected in their teaching.

John Henry Newman had a peculiarly receptive mind. It has often been observed of him that he had an uncanny knack, amounting almost to genius, of catching the spirit of a tradition, absorbing its ethos, and then—having partaken of such nourishment to his soul as the particular fount could supply—of imposing upon the teaching received his own distinctive interpretation, his own idiosyncratic twist; so that a mind which might at first appear to be that of an inspired eclectic reveals on closer inspection hidden depths of subtlety and originality, the stamp of the true philosopher who, while he learns from all who can teach him, is never content with an interpretation which is not his own. This is why Newman, who was not the originator of the Oxford Movement, nor —indeed by his own admission[12]—its primary theologian, was nevertheless the single genius which that movement threw up. John Keble inaugurated the movement and supplied the theological deposit, but it was Newman who gave it a perspective, who developed the original teaching into a distinctive ecclesiology, and who impressed his personality so deeply upon its concept of the religious life that Tractarianism could become more than an ephemeral manifestation of High Church pietism within the University of Oxford, but rather an enduring influence within the Anglican Church from 1830 to the present day.

Newman's was a restless mind, which always sought repose. In this he was utterly different from Keble. J. A. Froude has expressed the contrast thus:

> Newman's mind was world-wide. He was interested in everything which was going on in science, in politics, in literature. Nothing was too large for him, nothing too trivial, if it threw light upon the central question, what man really was, and what was his destiny. . . . Keble had looked into no lines of thought but his own. Newman had read omnivorously; he had studied modern thought and modern life in all its forms, and with all its many-coloured passions.[13]

The point should be taken further. All men have a certain number of natural or temperamental barriers which effectively prevent particular ideas or trains of thought impinging powerfully upon their minds. A man who is tone-deaf (as Keble was, as a matter of interest) will never succumb to the blandishments of music because his ear is insensitive to pitch. Certain intellectual appeals likewise will cause but a jangle and a discord in a man's mind if his temperament prevents him from making any sort of sense of the premisses. We all possess what J. B. Mozley, writing of the illative sense in Newman's *Grammar of Assent*, describes as certain "elementary convictions of the mind"[14] which determine our susceptibility to one argument and our incomprehension of another. Now Newman, receptive though he was, had such susceptibilities and mental blockages. He could not speak convincingly to an atheist, nor could he have been convinced by one.[15] It is doubtful whether he could have endured much converse with a liberal—by which he would mean a man who puts his faith in private judgement and who is therefore vulnerable to scepticism. For Newman the dogmatic principle, the recognition of an ultimate and infallible authority, was one of those "elementary convictions of the mind", induced by his conversion-experience at the age of fifteen and retained unshakably until the end of his life.[16]

Keble, by comparison, was a mass of these fundamental convictions. Whereas Newman went questing far and wide to find the dogmatic principle, Keble received it from his father and was satisfied. He imbibed the pure milk of the seventeenth-century divines, and asked for no other fare, save that on which the Caroline divines themselves had fed—the Fathers. The tradition had been passed from country parsonage to country parsonage, and in such an environment, the slow-moving and insulated Oxfordshire village of Fairford, Keble was left in his turn to guard the sacred deposit. He never went to school. He never, it seems, passed through a period of adolescence. As an undergraduate at Corpus he allowed no irreverent sally or dialectical engagement to ruffle his intellectual and spiritual composure. When rewarded with the highest academic prize that the University could offer—an Oriel Fellowship—he must have sat amidst the liveliest and sharpest minds in Oxford, feeling even as Newman did, and with less sound reason, "nunquam minus solus, quam cum solus".[17] It was not that he was priggish—a humbler man never lived. It was just that he had ceased to be receptive, and so he stopped his ears. This parochial, self-contained character remained with Keble to the end. He went abroad but once; when tempted to take a break, he would make for the seaside seclusion of Torquay.

Keble, then, represents the static element in the Oxford Movement, although he was not so obviously static as the old "High and Dry" Oxford tories like William Palmer of Worcester College, with whom on occasion the Tractarians might seem to walk in step. For Keble was, like Newman, a child of his times. Not even he could insulate himself against the prevailing mood of Romanticism, and indeed it penetrated to his very soul so that he must put his theology into verse and become, without realizing how exactly he had met the spirit of his time, the "sweet singer in our Israel".[18] In Keble natural reticence and reverence subdue the passions and suppress exuberance, so that a poem is both an emotional experience and an intellectual challenge, the more emotional because of the sense of sobriety, the more intellectually alluring because of the appeal to the past rather than to the present—to a past captured not by colourful detail but by opaque imagery and recondite allusion, supplying ethos rather than fact.

Now Newman could have concourse with a mind like that, and could and did receive much. But there is a dynamism in Newman which meant that he could not stay with Keble for long. It was a dynamism very different from that of Hurrell Froude. Froude was all impetuous energy, an ardent crusader in need of a cause. Left to himself, Christopher Dawson tells us, "Froude would have gone up like a rocket and left nothing behind him but a shower of sparks".[19] He needed ballast—a steadying force, someone who could both supply the cause and harness the energy. The coming-together of Keble and Froude in the Oxford reading-parties of the early 1820s was thus entirely felicitous to both parties, for Keble could never have taken upon himself without Froude's goading the role of a militant in delivering the Oxford Assize Sermon of 1833, with its bellicose text: "I will teach you the good and the right way". After Froude's early death in 1836 and the tragic change of direction which Newman appeared to be taking after 1841, Keble's brief period of active partisanship was over. As late as 1858 Keble had this interesting observation to make to Isaac Williams, thereby supplying the most revealing clue to his own role in the Oxford Movement that we possess:

> I look now upon my time with Newman and Pusey as a sort of parenthesis in my life; and I have now returned again to my old views such as I had before. At the time of the great Oxford Movement, when I used to go up to you at Oxford, Pusey and Newman were full of the wonderful progress and success of the movement—whereas I had always been taught that the truth must be unpopular and despised, and to make confession of it was all that one could do; but I see that I was fairly carried off my legs by the sanguine views they held, and the effects that were showing themselves in all quarters.[20]

The implications of this remark are very important indeed. To Keble the period when his teaching was taken up by younger men, developed and publicized in the *Tracts for the Times*, was really an irrelevance. He ought never to have allowed such a thing to happen; certainly he had failed in neglecting to dampen the ardour and banish the hopes of those who had sought to proselytize his views. He would return to the peaceful contemplation of forgotten truths, in no way shaken by the fact that the episcopate had seemed to declare against them. Keble could stop his ears even to bishops. He would be a St Basil, declaring "that God be true, though every man a liar".[21]

It was because of his perception of this rock-like composure in Keble, that Isaac Williams' account of the Oxford Movement in his *Autobiography* is so distinctive. It is the only history of Tractarianism which makes Keble the central figure. To Williams, who was always nearer to Keble than he was to Newman, the Oxford Movement had no inherent Romanizing tendency. No other substantial contributor to the *Tracts for the Times* felt the tensions that Newman was to feel. This was because there was always in Newman's allegiance to Tractarianism the desire to rove and to probe, which excited the occasional suspicion that he might only be a bird of passage. While Keble was content to demonstrate, Newman chose to put the Tractarian claims to the test. So it had ever been with Newman, and so it must always be. He knew where to seek the "Notes of the Church"; felt in his bones, one might say (for Newman was a thorough Romantic), what the proper ethos must be: there must be a continuing tradition of saints and martyrs, there must be the sanctity of the first ages, the mark of the apostolate: somewhere on her body the Church must bear the stigmata of Christ. Of all the wise observations of his life-long friend, R. W. Church, Dean of St Paul's, none was so penetrating as his final assessment of Newman's spiritual wanderings which he offered in the *Guardian* shortly after Newman's death:

> Form after form was tried by him, the Christianity of Evangelicalism, the Christianity of Whately, the Christianity of Hawkins, the Christianity of Keble and Pusey; it was all very well, but it was not the Christianity of the New Testament and of the first ages. He wrote *The Church of the Fathers* to show they were not merely evidence of religion, but really living men; that they could and did live as they taught, and what was there like the New Testament or even the first ages now? Alas! There was nothing completely like them. . . .[22]

Later—years later—when the spiritual journeyings were over and Newman came to review his long but consistent investigations into the relationship between Faith and Reason in *The Grammar of Assent*, he saw the Odyssey that he had been through as something necessary and inevitable, a series of mental and spiritual exercises, which mark the progress of the soul to Catholic truth. It conformed to what he came to describe as the "*organum investigandi* given us for gaining religious truth, and which would lead the mind by an infallible succession from the rejection of atheism to theism, and from theism to Christianity, and from Christianity to Evangelical Religion, and from these to Catholicity"[23]—a very teleological conception, we might say, as befitted an Oxford Aristotelian, but also a sentiment which betrays the conviction of the predestinarian, who knows that a hand is guiding him to the appointed end.

To Newman, then, the Oxford Movement was a phase in his spiritual progression; but he could not have so viewed it at the time, despite the suspicions of others; and the fact remains that during the time that he was the most active exponent of Tractarian teaching he contributed more to its theological insights than any other preacher or writer. Wherein, then, did Newman's originality lie?

His own answer was that he supplied little that was his own. Keble was the "true and primary author" of the Oxford Movement.[24] Keble had the creative mind. This self-effacing assessment can be well substantiated. In the main there were three leading ideas or lessons which Newman derived from Keble—an enduring respect, amounting to reverence, for the authority of the early

Published by J. Ryman

JOHN HENRY NEWMAN
PREACHING IN ST MARY'S OXFORD

George Richmond

JOHN KEBLE

Thomas Phillips

THOMAS ARNOLD

J. R. Story

MRS HUMPHREY WARD

Fathers; the consciousness of the true Catholic ethos, best conveyed by the medium of the doctrine of Reserve in Communicating Religious Knowledge; and, finally, an understanding of the role of the Church and the sacraments, utterly different from what he had encountered in the teaching of either the Evangelicals or of Richard Whately.

All three are of course related. In appreciating the one the inquiring mind will inevitably be led on to the others. But the Fathers come first. *In antiquis est scientia*—this was the first of Keble's lessons. One went back to the Caroline divines, to the continuators of the apostolic tradition who preserved the English Reformation from the errors of Continental Protestantism, and thence to the sources of their own inspiration, the Fathers themselves. What, in fact, did this mean? It brought one into a world of saints and martyrs which had an instant appeal to the Romantic mind. It was not only that this world antedated the alleged corruptions of the Roman Communion—papal infallibility, mariolatry, invocation of saints, transubstantiation and the like—and therefore represented most faithfully the apostolicity, the spirit of primitive purity, which the Tractarians (they called themselves "Apostolicals" as their chosen party label) sought to recover in the Church of their own day. It was the ethos of these times which touched the heart: having an epic, heroic quality—mighty deeds, self-sacrifice unto death, a sort of total theological involvement, which the Tractarians craved to emulate. Newman, Nicholas Wiseman, and Robert Wilberforce all chose this setting for novels,[25] a setting which, one would have to admit, would seem from the point of view of the present day a little unpropitious. Much of this was Romantic idealism, but the intensity and desire to aspire to these heights was real enough. The celibacy cult of the Newman circle in the late 1820s, for instance (which Sir Geoffrey Faber so completely misunderstood in a controversial chapter of his controversial book, with hints of Freudian sublimations and homosexual proclivities),[26] is the most obvious example of this. The nature of the times, and the state of the Church, demanded that a group of dedicated men should set such an example of self-sacrifice by deliberately choosing the celibate state, that "high state of life", as Newman himself put it, "to which the multitude of men cannot aspire".[27]

All through his life, after his friendship with Keble began, Newman took the early Fathers as his primary source. His first published work was a history of the Arians,[28] followed by a series of articles on "The Church of the Fathers" published in the

British Magazine between 1833 and 1836. In the first of these articles, Newman stated his grand design to be to demonstrate "the power of the Church at that time, and on what it was based, not (as Protestants imagine) on governments, or on human law, or on endowments, but on popular enthusiasm, on dogma, on hierarchical power, and on a supernatural Divine Presence".[29] What it once was, so must it always strive to be. Such was the argument of the *Essay on Development*, Newman's gift to the Roman Catholic Church, a book as perplexing to his new co-religionists as it was to his old. The argument throughout is patristic, not Thomist or Tridentine; and he turned the tables on his Tractarian colleagues of old by arguing the Roman claims from the very sources which Anglicans were confidently using to repudiate them.[30] In his sermons, Newman constantly brought forward the patristic ideal:

> How unlike are the best among us to the Saints and Martyrs of old time; to St Cyprian, or St Basil, or St Ambrose, or St Leo! and what an utter mockery it is to couple their names with modern names, and to compare their words with our words, as is sometimes done! yet, if true love be the tie that binds us to them, since they most certainly cannot move towards us, we through God's mercy perchance may be drawn to them.[31]

It is in *The Arians of the Fourth Century* that Newman developed most fully the second of the great truths which he derived from Keble, namely the doctrine of Reserve in Communicating Religious Knowledge, perhaps the most significant element in Tractarian teaching, for it takes us to the very bedrock of its theology and ecclesiology. Just as the appeal to the Fathers touched both heart and head, by evoking a sense of ethos and encouraging the study of dogma, so this particular tenet of patristic teaching contained implications both doctrinal and emotional. There is the doctrine itself, the *disciplina arcani*, most fully analysed from scriptural, patristic, and more recent sources by Isaac Williams in Tracts 80 and 87: and there was the concept of religious life which that doctrine implies—the form of religiosity which it engenders. Both aspects are of supreme importance for an understanding of Tractarianism and the Oxford Movement.

The meaning of the doctrine is simply this—there is, as the Epistle to the Hebrews indicates, a distinction between the teaching which is appropriate for the weak and ignorant and that which is the property of a baptized and regenerate Christian. There are some to whom the mysteries must be told in parables; they need "the nourishment of children rather than of grown men".[32] "Only the pure in heart shall see God." In the words of Justin Martyr, "Knowledge is not safe without a true life."[33] This was the assumption of the early catechetical schools: to become one of the Competantes or Electi, the catechumens must learn in easy stages until they were fit to receive the most sacred verities. Now this at once postulates an understanding of the role of the Church *vis-à-vis* the revelation contained in the Scriptures to which good Protestants must object. Newman puts it thus:

> Surely the sacred volume was never intended and is not adapted to teach us our creed; however certain it is that we can prove our creed from it, where it has once been taught us, and in spite of individual produceable exceptions to the general rule. From the very first, the rule has been, as a matter of fact, for the Church to teach the truth, and then appeal to Scripture in vindication of its own teaching.[34]

The plainest meaning of the doctrine, however, is to supply the justification for religious teaching through accommodation. What is taught by the Church is accommodated to the moral and intellectual state of those whom it is instructing. Now this was not necessarily a High Church doctrine. Indeed the fullest exposition of the necessity of accommodation, in the writings of that time, comes from the pen of Thomas Arnold in his *Essay on the Right Interpretation and Understanding of the Scriptures.*

> The revelations of God to man were gradual [he wrote] and adapted to his state at the several periods when they were successively made. And on the same principle commands were given at one time which were not given at another; and which, according to God's method of dealing with mankind, not only were not *but could not have been given.* This brings us to the famous doctrine of accommodation, which, having been carried by some persons to an extravagant and offensive length, has fallen, consequently, with many good men, into great suspicion.

He then referred to the error of the Nicolaitans, and continued: "I am not considering how a wicked man may pervert this doctrine but how a good man may profit from it".[35]

What Arnold was defending here was the notion of progressive revelation, argued from the *Kenosis* of Christ himself (i.e. "it is manifest that Infinity, thus communing with his finite creatures, must have adapted himself to their notions"),[36] with the implication that as men grow through time and the accumulation of knowledge and deeper spiritual insight so God will reveal more of himself and his purposes, so that an informed believer of the nineteenth century will possess greater knowledge of God than one of the original apostles. Such an implication would have been abhorrent to Keble and Newman. Their emphasis was on the need at any time for the Church to conceal or to disguise the sacred truths of which it was the guardian, in case "pearls should be cast before swine"; and it was precisely this attitude, which might take the form of teaching by half-truths or appealing to superstitious and ignorant credulity, that Charles Kingsley attacked, on the notorious occasion in 1864, when he accused Newman of teaching that "truth is no virtue", thereby provoking perhaps the most celebrated riposte in the whole history of theological conflict.

One thing, however, is clear. Accommodation might mean one thing to Arnold and quite a different thing to Newman; but it meant nothing to the Evangelicals. It contradicted the fundamental article of their creed—the compulsion to preach the Gospel to every living creature; more than that, it denoted an attitude towards the religious life—a sobriety and secretiveness of disposition, a self-conscious austerity of manner and approach—which was the very antithesis of the accepted pattern of Evangelical behaviour and demeanour. A man converted—a *real* Christian, a *serious* Christian—was a man noticeably in love with his Redeemer. He wore his heart for ever on his sleeve. He was a man who exuded Christian joy—like Wilberforce, who seemed already in Heaven while on earth, who spoke of biblical figures and the saints as if he had known them personally and they were his constant friends and companions.

Newman could never have been an Evangelical for long: the exuberance and religiosity were repugnant to him. For this reason he was temperamentally disposed to find in Keble, with his horror of enthusiasm and his natural reticence, a kindred spirit, and to feel at once the emotional appeal of the doctrine of Reserve. This doctrine certainly had a place for the heart. Had it not been so, it could never have supplied the spiritual needs and longings of a group of Romantics. But it avoided, indeed repudiated, the two great perils which Newman saw to be the gravest defects in the Evangelical religion of his day. In the first place, Evangelicals laid too great a stress on the role of feeling as a test of growth in grace, thereby betraying a naive subjectivism in their understanding of religious experience. This was anathema to Newman (particularly so, one suspects, because of his own enduring conversion experience and the subsequent temptation to fall into this snare). "Religion, as a mere sentiment," he wrote in the *Apologia*, "is to me a dream and a mockery."[37] And again, more fully, in his concluding paragraph to Tract 73 ("On the introduction of rationalistic principles in Religion") he indicates the dangers thus:

> I will conclude by summing up in one sentence, which must be pardoned me, if in appearance harsh, what the foregoing discussion is intended to show. There is a widely spread though variously admitted school of doctrine among us, within and without the Church, which intends and professes peculiar piety, as directing its attention to the *heart itself*, not to any thing external to us, whether creed, actions, or ritual. I do not hesitate to assert that this doctrine is based upon error, that it is really a specious form of trusting man rather than God, that it is in its nature Rationalistic, and that it tends to Socinianism. How the individual supporters of it will act as time goes on is another matter, the good will be separated from the bad; but the School as such will pass through Sabellianism to that "God-denying Apostasy", to use the ancient phrase, to which in the beginning of its career it professed itself to be especially opposed.[38]

The second peril of Evangelical emotionalism was that their familiarity, in their mode of address on things divine, would lead to contempt. It would both cheapen the mysterious truths themselves by vulgarizing them in histrionic sermons addressed to the masses, and it would reduce their content into cant by converting the most solemn truths that could hardly be uttered without blasphemy into pious catchphrases and slogans repeated *ad nausean* supposedly for mutual edification. Newman explained his feelings on this very plainly in a letter to James Stephen in 1835. While he respected the great pioneers of the Evangelical Revival he could not endure

> their rudeness, irreverence, and almost profaneness. . . . The poorest and humblest ought to shrink from the irreverence necessarily involved in pulpit addresses, which speak of the adorable works and sufferings of Christ with the familiarity and absence of awe with which we speak about our friends. Zaccheus did not intrude himself on our Lord—the woman that was a sinner *silently* bedewed his feet. Which of us is less refined than "a tax-gatherer or a harlot"? Would not either of these be inexpressibly distressed to hear the commonplace, mechanical way in which the great doctrine of his sacred death and the benefit of his blood-shedding is thrown to and fro, at best as if a spell or charm, which would surely convert man?[39]

Keble felt this too. The sobriety and austerity with which he dealt with holy things did not betoken a want of love. Far from it. The love that he bore was so precious that it was guarded and concealed, cherished in the utmost intimacy, never paraded or noised abroad. This attitude is best seen in Keble's approach to poetry. Poetry had to Keble almost a sacramental character—it was a means of conveying the deepest and most sacred truths by veiled allusions and subtle imagery, so that only those fit to receive them could fully understand.[40] So deeply did he feel this that he went so far as to defend the practice of the Professor of Poetry at Oxford lecturing in Latin on the esoteric nature of his art in order to ensure that the secrets were not divulged to the unworthy.[41] As early as 1825 in the *Quarterly Review* he indicated his distaste for Milton because "it was the temper of the man always to speak out. He carried it to a faulty excess"; whereas Spenser (his favourite poet) commanded "a shrinking delicacy" which always kept him back, "through fear of profaning things hallowed by an unworthy touch".[42]

I have dealt at some length with the doctrine of Reserve because, more than anything else, it explains the ethos of the Oxford Movement and the Tractarian theology. It also reflects most faithfully the kinship between Keble and Newman, who were united in their recognition of the centrality of this doctrine as representing the Catholic and Apostolic elements most lacking in the Church of their day. More important, however, is the way in which this doctrine shaped the ecclesiology and, arising from this, the sacramental theology of the Tractarians. It is in this sphere that the originality of Newman himself primarily lies, and it constitutes his greatest individual contribution to the Oxford Movement.

There is room for dispute here, of course. Some will say that Newman's finest intellectual achievement lay in the field of epistemology—his analysis of the relationship between faith and reason as worked out in the Oxford University Sermons and finally in *The Grammar of Assent.* I should not quarrel with this, but say that this was in a sense irrelevant to the Oxford Movement and formed no essential part of Tractarian theology. Even in the realm of sacramental theology Newman's contribution must be reckoned less than that of E. B. Pusey and R. I. Wilberforce, although their own elaboration of the sacramental system and the nature of the Eucharist was consonant with, if not actually developed from, Newman's treatment of the subject in the *Lectures on Justification.* Furthermore, much of the ecclesiology itself was by its very nature dated, since it was concerned with the construction of a *via media* between Romanism and popular Protestantism, which the author himself came within ten years to discard as unsatisfactory. As Monsignor Davis has put it, "It would be gratifying to be able to say that Newman has had an influence on the course and character of British theology. Yet it would be unrealistic to see this influence in any province but that of a certain dated Church of England ecclesiology."[43]

But something remains; and this is found not in the most obvious sources—the *Prophetical Office of the Church* and the final exposition of *via media* theology in a more pronounced Roman sense in *Tract 90*—but rather in the less polemical sermons. Newman's most eloquent and most significant writing on the nature of the Church appears in the sermon on "Christian Nobleness" preached as early as 22 May 1831. In this the doctrine of Reserve is translated into ecclesiological terms; the religiosity of the Oxford Movement as contrasted with that of the Evangelicals receives its classic expression.

"The Apostles' fellowship with Christ through the Spirit, after his ascension, was very different from their fellowship with him on earth," he writes. He then alludes to Christ's own words about the unforgivable sin of speaking against the Holy Ghost. He refers to St Paul: "Work out your own salvation with fear and trembling", "Grieve not the Holy Spirit of God". Then follows this great passage:

> This great truth is impressed upon the whole course of that sacred fellowship with Christ, which the Church provides for her children; in proportion as it is more high and gracious than that first intercourse which the Apostles enjoyed, so is it also more awful. When He had once ascended, henceforth for unstudied speech there were solemn rites; for familiar attendance there were mysterious ministerings; for questioning at will there was silent obedience; for sitting at table there was bowing in adoration; for eating and drinking there was feasting and watching. He who had taken his Lord and rebuked Him dared not speak to Him after His resurrection, when he saw and knew Him. He who had lain in His bosom at supper fell at His feet as dead. Such was the vision of the glorified Saviour of man, returning to His redeemed in the power of the spirit with a Presence more pervading because more intimate, and more real because more hidden. And as the manner of His coming was new, so was His gift. It was peace, but a new peace, "not as the world giveth", not the exultation of the young, light-hearted and simple, easily created, easily lost; but a serious, sober, lasting comfort, full of reverence, deep in contemplation.[44]

The Church, then, is the medium for contact between finite and infinite. Where once the Lord had spoken to man in common speech, now—after the Redemption—the Spirit communicates through the sacraments. They are the prescribed channels. The joy of spontaneous communication is banished. In its stead must be the sobriety and reverence which accompany the most solemn functions which the Church is empowered to perform—the safeguarding of the means of grace.

Never suppose that Newman, for all his mastery of the written and spoken word, preached a popular message. He might hold a packed congregation in his sway, gripped in a silence through the long pauses which punctuated every sentence, such as that experienced by the soul of Gerontius hearing "no more the busy beat of time". But his purpose was to engender fear and penitence. As he once observed to Samuel Wilberforce: "We require the Law not the Gospel in this age. We want rousing, we want the claims of duty and the details of obedience set before us strongly." And again, "We require the Law's stern fires. We need a continual Ash Wednesday."[45] The mass of men were deluded into supposing that respectability was synonymous with sanctification, that a thorough and heart-felt repentance might be left to the death-bed. Newman's rejoinder is simple: "Heaven would be Hell to an irreligious man."[46]

The Church may represent the beauty of holiness. It was one of his major criticisms of the Church of his own day that it showed insufficient awareness of the yearning for Catholic externals, of the importance of satisfying "the needs of the heart".[47] But above all, it must inculcate the true apostolical ethos of severity.

" 'All is not gold that glitters' as the proverb goes; and all is not Catholic and Apostolical which effects what is high and beautiful and speaks to the imagination. Religion has two sides, a severe side, and a beautiful; and we shall be sure to swerve from the narrow way which leads to life, if we indulge ourselves in what is beautiful while we put aside what is severe."[48]

Now this is the point; and it is our final point. The way to life is "narrow", the most important constituent of Christianity is that it is "severe". The Church is not an Establishment, providing a respectable profession for "smug parsons" with "pony-carriages for their wives and daughters". [49] This is what the Oxford Movement was chiefly about; and it was Newman's unique role to proclaim this particular message with an emotional power which none perhaps before or since has ever equalled. And herein, too, will be found the real reasons why Newman left the Church of his baptism at the cost of a broken heart. I have argued elsewhere that the narrowness of the way to life as worked out in Newman's theology of the 1830s was such that he came to plot a *via media* between Rome and continental Protestantism which was impossible for all but the saints to travel, because he enjoined Christians to attain sanctification while rejecting the means and the comforts which the rival systems had devised. He would not count good works as meritorious, and he could not accept final perseverance.[50] But it was not this that moved Newman in the end; it was not his way to look for easier routes. If his main contribution to the Oxford Movement had been to develop an ecclesiology, his translation "to another portion of the Lord's vineyard" came about because he put that ecclesiology to the test. In the end he asked himself this question—which of the two Churches, the Anglican or the Roman, bore the enduring marks of the apostolic age, so that it would be immediately recognized as the true Church by one of the saints of old, should he be permitted to return to earth?

He put the position thus to one who was still wavering—A. J. Hamner—in November 1849: "To my mind the overbearingly convincing proof is this—that were St Athanasius or St Ambrose in London now, they would go to worship, not to St Paul's Cathedral, but to Warwick Street or Moor Fields. This my own reading of history has made to me an axiom, and it converted me, though I cannot of course communicate the force of it to another." Newman must go to where the ethos of the fourth and fifth centuries is preserved still, where yet there remain "altars, tombs, pilgrimages, processions, rites, relics, medals, etc. I hardly see a trace of the Church of the Fathers, as a living acting being, in the Anglican communion."[51]

"Look on this picture and on that." Looking to the Roman Church, Newman now recognized what he had sought—"the movement of my spiritual mother *Incessu patuit Dea*".[52]

Not everyone would come to the same conclusion. It is an essentially subjective judgement. One looks for what one feels to have been the ethos of the Church of old, one tastes what the flavour of sanctity must have been. It is interesting and something of a paradox that, while Newman rejected Evangelicalism because it made feeling a test of growth in grace, he appears in the end to have accepted Romanism because he made feeling, above all else, the crucial test for discerning the identity of the one true Church. The Oxford Movement had been primarily a movement of the heart. Newman's conversion was too.

NOTES

1. MS. letter from Robert Carr to R. I. Wilberforce, quoted in my *The Parting of Friends* (1966), p. 15.
2. A. Mozley (ed.), *Letters and Correspondence of John Henry Newman* (1891), Letter 204.
3. M. Pattison, *Memoirs* (1885), p. 236.
4. R. W. Church, *The Oxford Movement, Twelve Years 1833–1845* (1891), pp. 139–41.

5. T. Mozley, *Reminiscences chiefly of Oriel College and the Oxford Movement* (1882), I, p. 313.
6. These were the Bampton Lectures of 1832, entitled "Scholastic Philosophy considered in its relation to Christian Theology". See H. P. Lidden, *Life of E. B. Pusey* (1854), I, pp. 361–4.
7. J. H. Newman, *Apologia pro vita sua*. Wilfred Ward's edition (1913), p. 267.
8. This was Thomas Arnold. See my *The Parting of Friends*, p. 165.
9. William Palmer, *A Narrative of Events connected with the Publication of the Tracts for the Times* (1883), p. 99.
10. Y. Brilioth, *Evangelicalism and the Oxford Movement: Three Lectures* (1934), p. 28.
11. See my *The Parting of Friends*, p. 316.
12. J. H. Newman, *Apologia*, p. 119.
13. J. A. Froude, *Short Studies on Great Subjects* (1891), IV, pp. 278–80.
14. J. B. Mozley, *Lectures and other Theological Papers* (1883), p. 281.
15. See the argument, full of self-revelatory detail, in J. H. Newman, *A Grammar of Assent* (1906 edn), pp. 415–18.
16. *Apologia*, p. 150.
17. Ibid. p. 118.
18. From a MS letter of John Sargent to Samuel Wilberforce; see my *The Parting of Friends. A Study of the Wilberforce and Henry Manning* (1966), p. 85.
19. Christopher Dawson, *The Spirit of the Oxford Movement* (1945), p. 16.
20. Sir G. Prevost (ed.), *The Autobiography of Isaac Williams* (2nd edn, 1892), p. 118, note 1.
21. MS letter of John Keble to R. I. Wilberforce, quoted in *The Parting of Friends*, p. 394.
22. R. W. Church, *Occasional Papers* (1897), II, pp. 472–3.
23. J. H. Newman, *Grammar of Assent*, Note II, p. 499.
24. J. H. Newman, *Apologia*, pp. 119–29.
25. J. H. Newman, *Callista* (1855); Nicholas Wiseman, *Fabiola* (1854); R. I. Wilberforce, *Rutilius and Lucius* (1842).
26. Geoffrey Faber, *Oxford Apostles* (1933), chapter VI, "Secret Forces".
27. Newman in a letter to G. D. Ryder, see *The Parting of Friends*, p. 153.
28. J. H. Newman, *The Arians of the Fourth Century: their Doctrine, Temper and Conduct* (1833).
29. J. H. Newman, *Historical Sketches* (1872), II, p. 342.
30. See especially, Owen Chadwick, *From Bossuet to Newman. The Idea of Doctrinal Development* (Cambridge, 1957), pp. 143–4.
31. J. H. Newman, *Sermons bearing on Subjects of the Day* (1918 edn), p. 390.
32. J. H. Newman, *Arians*, p. 47.
33. Isaac Williams, "On Reserve in Communicating Religious Knowledge", Part I, *Tract 80* (1835) in *Tracts for the Times* IV, p. 61.
34. J. H. Newman, op. cit., 55–6.
35. Thomas Arnold, "Essay on the Right Interpretation and Understanding of the Scriptures" in *Sermons*, II (1878 edn), p. 285.
36. Ibid. 286–7.
37. J. H. Newman, *Apologia*, p. 150.
38. J. H. Newman, "On the Introduction of Rationalistic Principles into Religion", Tract 73 (1835), p. 53 in *Tract for the Times* III.
39. See my article, "Justification and Sanctification: Newman and the Evangelicals" in *Journal of Theological Studies* NS Vol. XV, Part I (1964), pp. 49–50.
40. See Walter Lock, *John Keble* (1893), p. 48.
41. E. K. Francis, *Keble's Lectures on Poetry 1832–1841* (1912), I. Inaugural Lecture as Professor of Poetry.
42. John Keble, *Occasional Papers and Reviews* (1877), pp. 102–3.
43. H. Francis Davis, "Newman's influence in England" in *The Rediscovery of Newman*, ed. by John Coulson and A. M. Allchin (1967), p. 216.

44. J. H. Newman, *Sermons on Subjects of the Day*, pp. 140–1.
45. *Journal of Theological Studies*, NS Vol. XV.I, op. cit. pp. 43, 45.
46. J. H. Newman, *Parochial and Plain Sermons* (1868 edn), I, p. 7.
47. E. S. Purcell, *Life of Cardinal Manning* (1896), I, p. 233.
48. J. H. Newman, *Sermons on Subjects of the Day*, p. 391.
49. R. W. Church, *Occasional Papers*, II, p. 473.
50. In *Journal of Theological Studies* op. cit., p. 53; *The Parting of Friends*, pp. 209–10.
51. *Letters and Diaries of John Henry Newman*, ed. C. S. Dessein, XIII (1963), pp. 295–6.
52. J. H. Newman, *Apologia*, p. 132.

5

The Established Church under Attack

OWEN CHADWICK

The larger part of the question posed by the title I have been given touches an area which the historian can illustrate but cannot analyse. The influence of moral ideals upon a person is not something which the person himself can chart or fathom, still less his friends, still less the analyst dependent on written sources. *A fortiori* the influence of the same ideals upon a large group of persons, or a nation, can only be given illustrations. George Lansbury attributed his socialist principles to his upbringing in the Church of England. It is difficult to doubt that in some respect or other Christianity contributed to Lansbury's socialism, but we are not able to define in what respect, or distinguish such an influence from the influence of (let us say) a Marxist like Hyndman, even if we have some evidence that the moral element in his nature was the strongest of the forces that made him a politician. Dr Barnardo believed that he was under the direct leading of God in the work that he did for waifs and that without God he would never have done it. It cannot be doubted that the Christian drive of the Victorians included a drive to save and to better the poor and the sick. Christianity was integral to the ideals and the work of countless reformers, from Florence Nightingale or Sister Dora or Josephine Butler or Dora Greenwell to Quintin Hogg and Samuel Barnett and W. E. Gladstone. We cannot of course tell how far they were Christians because they were good men and how far they were good men because they were Christians. But certainly it was in part the second of these. For some of them set out to "convert", and in the process found themselves rescuing from disease or starvation or prostitution or illiteracy, until the rescuing became much more their work than the converting. The career of the Salvation Army, which began as a preaching revival and turned into a force among tramps and drunks, is typical of much social endeavour during that age. "I know no Liberalism", Arthur Stanton was wont to say, "except that which I have sucked in from the breasts of the gospel";[1] and we are not able to speculate how far he was right in his self-examination, and how much he owed to schoolmasters or to an admiration for Gladstone.

The Church of England was under attack, first, because it was one of the Churches and all Churches were under attack throughout the reign of Queen Victoria. But the attacks at the end of the reign looked different from the attacks at the beginning.

In 1837 the Churches were attacked by the pamphleteers of the working men, heirs of Tom Paine and the political programme of the French Revolution. These pamphleteers were sometimes blasphemers and for the most part ignorant, fanatical, and easy to disregard. Authority did not always disregard them. When Sir Robert Peel was Prime Minister the Archbishop of Canterbury (8 January 1842) wrote to him about the problem of atheist pamphleteers and Peel gave little hope of action by the Government, for the Government would only sell the pamphlets if it prosecuted.[2] But many of these working-class pamphlets the Government was able to treat almost as it treated obscenities. The pamphlets had no sort of influence on any of the citizens who were educated and on few of those who possessed a vote.

A lot of the attacks on the Churches towards the end of the reign came from the ideological and social descendants of the working-class pamphleteers. Modern research tends to show more continuity in the tradition than might have been predicted. But in the 90s the working-class pamphleteers had the vote, and far more education was accessible to the writers, and thanks to national education an incomparably larger public of working men was capable of reading what they wrote. The Churches believed in education and always strove to improve it. But just occasionally their less wise members lamented that advancing education merely made it possible for the uneducated to read anti-Christian books.

Therefore the attack of working-class culture upon the Churches, though in essence the same attack early or late, was more powerful in 1890 than in 1840. For it was with better weapons and could reach the furthest village in the land. It was far from being treatable as pornography now. Part of it was serious argument and a little of it was sober inquiry, and some of it might be bought on a bookstall at the station.

And yet the working man was not deeply moved by these activities. Most observers agreed that the Churches and the parsons puzzled him or passed him by, but did not anger him. He sometimes had an obscure feeling that the church worker was an unconscious agent of the Conservative party or even of the police, and he often supposed that ministers, like other members of the leisured classes, did no work that could be called work. But usually he was indifferent and not hostile. Observers noticed that he was apathetic to nearly every other interest that was not connected with his daily bread. In the midst of his apathy he felt inarticulately that the world was unjust to him and that these kind parsons were mysteriously associated with the injustice.

For by the last decades of the century the pamphleteers, failing to persuade the masses to resent either Christianity or its official representatives, succeeded in injecting into the consciousness of the poor a powerful idea: the preachers contribute to injustice by the promise of future rewards. *Suffer here and you shall be crowned hereafter*—resignation into the hands of God was central to the Christian ethic. Are we to be content with our lot when that lot is inflicted upon us by the robbery sanctioned under the laws of property? "We want," Karl Marx's daughter said in the refreshment room of the British Museum, "to make them [the masses] disregard the mythical next world and live for this world, and insist on having what will make it pleasant to them."[3] The working man was told that the doctrine of the future life was not only a doubtful truth but a dangerous lie, a way of keeping him down. In the East London of the 90s he began to use the contemptuous phrase (in its origin without the affection with which it became used in the slang of the twentieth century) "sky pilot" to describe a Christian minister. Down into the villages went "secularist" lecturers who stood on the green and told the people of the untruths of Christianity and of the social ills fostered by the Churches. A secularist shoemaker settled in a village and offered lectures on Sunday and converted at least one mother to the belief that she had been wrong to take her children to be baptized in church.

And yet the country, even at the end of the Queen's reign, was still in many respects a deeply Christian country. Nothing is more remarkable than the religiousness of the early leaders of the Labour movement when they wanted to capture the political allegiance of working men. The early writings and speeches of Keir Hardie or Ramsay Macdonald or Philip Snowden or George Lansbury not merely show that the religious and moral ideal was integral to their own conception of socialism, and that they had little use for the cruder doctrines of "opium of the people". They tend to show that a religiousness of mood and language was politically desirable; that is, that they would be more likely to be heard by the audience which they sought, if they dissociated socialism from its continental atmosphere of class warfare and revolution and associated it with Christian ideas of fraternity and care for the poor. That did not mean to say that they did not attack the Churches. Their attack upon the Churches was often bitter and extreme. But, like some of the early Chartists, they were more likely to attack the Churches because they were unrepresentative of Christianity than because they represented it. They assailed the Christians because they failed to follow Christ, not because they sought to follow him. They sometimes sought to show that in modern society the programme of socialism was a necessary outcome of Christian ideals.

Keir Hardie's family deserted the Church when he was young because they associated (Presbyterian) churchmen with middle-class and hypocritical and unjust conduct. In later days Hardie would preach in Methodist pulpits or in Labour churches, or associate himself with the theosophists or the Pleasant Sunday Afternoon. When the T.U.C. met at Norwich in 1894 many of them walked in the close at sunset; and, as they heard Psalm 23 sung by the worshippers inside the cathedral, it was Hardie who led them all off, Christians and agnostics, to join in the song—"not so much in any devotional spirit as out of deference to the influence of the place".[4] He once puzzled a mass audience of continental socialists in the square at Lille by telling them, "I myself have found in the Christianity of Christ the inspiration which first of all drove me into the movement and has carried me on in it".[5]

But he could be bitterer than anyone else about the hired professors of Christianity. His Christmas message in the *Labour Leader* for 1897 was unparalleled for bitterness among Christmas messages.

Although many more people did not go to church or chapel than in the early Victorian age, it must never be forgotten that many more people did go to church or chapel than in the early Victorian age. The country was far more populous. Thus we have the curious paradox, which may now be regarded as proven statistically, that the Churches had a wonderful sense of expansion and well-being during years when they were failing to keep pace with the growth of population. To understand this is necessary to the understanding of Victorian "secularization". The statistics

William Rothenstein

LESLIE STEPHEN

Illustrated London News

AN EVENING SERVICE IN WESTMINSTER ABBEY IN MARCH 1861

prove that during the last twenty years of the century the Churches were losing significantly, if to "lose" is equivalent to a failure to expand by the same percentage as the population of the country was expanding. On this basis of percentages modern books have criticized the Victorian Churches for their "failure". But the Victorian Churches themselves had no such notions. They saw a great task in front of them, in the rapid urbanization of England and Wales, and made extraordinary endeavour to meet the need, and felt modestly rewarded. They might see country congregations declining, but they could see town congregations growing larger or (more commonly) subdividing in remarkable ways. What they cared for was their obvious growth. The increase of Christian worshippers was more evident to them than the increase in the total numbers of the people.

The sense of expanding numbers was often accompanied, during the 80s and 90s, by another feeling, that of increasing influence in the State. The phrase "the nonconformist conscience" was originally a phrase of abuse during the affair of Parnell's fall, and was adopted by the Methodist minister Hugh Price Hughes as a term of compliment. The phrase stood for an obvious truth; that the political power of nonconformity, between 1867 and 1905, was a force to be reckoned with. This political power must not be understood merely as one of the forces behind the electoral successes of the Liberal party. Its existence helped to condition public attitudes to moral issues, such as temperance, or prostitution, or Sunday observance, or Bulgarian massacres, or concentration camps in South Africa, or oppression in the Congo. It brought the strong conscience of the middle classes to bear upon national questions, sometimes in an emotional way, but seldom in a way which politicians could afford to disregard. Not all its manifestations, when based upon an ill-informed emotion, were equally moral. But "the nonconformist conscience" was neither exclusively nor even generally nonconformist. It was one aspect of a force which Bernard Shaw would later pillory as "middle-class morality", but which on its better side displayed and developed the influence of the Churches in the public life of the nation. Archbishop Benson of Canterbury declared in 1893 that everyone saw how the influence of the Churches had increased during the last twenty years. Far more children were being taught the Christian religion in 1890 than in 1850. It was true that the universities of Oxford and Cambridge and Durham, and King's College, London, were prised apart from the Church of England by a series of Acts of Parliament between 1854 and 1899. But most people able to make comparisons believed that Oxford and Cambridge universities were more encouraging to the religion of their undergraduates in 1890 than twenty-five years before. Two of the three Prime Ministers of the last twenty years of the reign (Gladstone and Salisbury) were far more Christian than the first Prime Minister of the reign. At the highest level of political life we cannot easily find that the attacks upon Christianity diminished the influence of the established Church or of any other Church.

In the realm of ideas we find far more uncertainty.

If Christianity included a belief that the world was 6,000 years old and not more, or that Jonah was swallowed by a whale, then Christianity was proved untrue, and its influence must diminish and vanish as society progressively realized its falsehood. And since some people believed that the geologists or Darwin or Colenso had "disproved the Bible", those people also believed that the philosophy which alone justified the Churches was obsolescent.

But not many intelligent people did believe this. They perceived that Christianity had other content besides various pieces of historical information with which it was hitherto often associated. It is not at all easy to find a Victorian who "lost his faith" because he discovered that Genesis chapter 1 was not literally true. One highly intelligent Victorian, Leslie Stephen, is sometimes represented as losing his faith because he could no longer believe in a universal flood. He did this during the 60s when for thirty years most educated men had ceased to believe in a universal flood. It is impossible to suppose, despite Stephen's biographer, that he took orders in the Church of England with a total and unquestioning faith in a universal flood. From Stephen's own descriptions we sense a more subtle attitude. It was less a question of intellectual dissent than of moral repudiation. Here was he, a clergyman who did not believe in stories in the Bible, placed by his Church in a situation where the liturgy compelled him to read such stories as though they were true. He could do it no longer. He could not assume, as his successors could assume, that the congregation would not for one moment suppose him to take the story of Noah to be history.

But if it is not easy to point to individuals in intellectual difficulty over particulars it is easy to illustrate the general unsettlement of ideas arising from new knowledge. Victorian doubt should be judged less by the leaders of the argument than by schoolboys who heard vaguely that Darwin proved the Bible not to be true. And the difficulty was not made easier, either by the aggressiveness of a few scientists like Huxley and Tyndall, or by the obscurantism of some clergymen, from Cardinal Manning downwards, who asserted the incompatibility between Christianity and doctrines of Evolution.

How far this general unsettlement weakened the Churches it is not at all easy to determine, or to see what evidence would enable us to make a precise estimate. The statistics of London and of Lancashire, two of the few places where we have fairly reliable statistics, show that in the last fifteen or twenty years of the century the number of worshippers ceased to rise, not merely per cent of the population, but absolutely, and began to fall. We have a little, too haphazard, evidence that the persons sometimes known as "nothingarians"—adherents of no denomination—began to rise in the same period. It is necessary to remember that this may be more the result of social conditions than of intellectual, and yet difficult to imagine it as altogether unconnected with the militancy of a Huxley, the liberal divinity of a Matthew Arnold, the rumours about Colenso—or, above all, with the circumstance that no open-eyed man of 1890 could read the Bible in the same attitude as it was read by most men fifty years before.

What on present evidence looks probable is that changes in social conditions were more important than new knowledge in changing religious practice. There have been preliminary attempts to distinguish between the effects of related but cognate developments, like urbanization and industrialization.

We may provisionally distinguish:

1. Change of habitat; certainly important in breaking habits of churchgoing; and more people than ever before in English history were changing their place of dwelling.

2. Change of habitat to a place where the individual was lost in a crowd and his individuality less evident, and his neglect of custom unperceived.

3. Change in manner of work, from work associated with a rural economy to work associated with an urban economy—and there is as yet no reliable evidence that this was important, though this is not to say that it was not.

4. Change in relationship to the employer, from one of personal service to one of contract. Some Victorian observers, concerned about the declining churchgoing of the rural labourer after the agricultural troubles of the 70s, were inclined to diagnose that this change was important. In crude terms, the farmer's employee used to go to church because the farmer went and he stood in a

personal relation to the farmer. Few men working in a mill thought of going to church because the mill-owner set him an example. On present information, however, we are not able adequately to test whether this contemporary feeling was justified. Some of those who lamented the fall in the churchgoing of the rural labourer were inclined to adopt hazy and utopian pictures of the villages before the troubles of agriculture afflicted them. A little evidence has been produced that villages where the property was parcelled out in freeholds were less likely to produce numerous worshippers than villages where the squire owned all the property and the inhabitants (or most of them) were his tenants. If further investigation confirms this, it would be a striking pointer towards the Victorian belief that the squire's example and influence were very important to the moral and religious behaviour of the village; and that the decline of the squire, in the general decline of agriculture and the landowning interest, was of consequence for the welfare of the established Church in the country districts.

Here then we have two great facts troubling the Churches: a general shaking and revision of all accepted ideas by an extraordinary influx of new knowledge, scientific and historical; and a vast movement of population, creating new ways of life and uprooting the landmarks of centuries. The Churches, which by the nature of their liturgical function could not adjust their thought or their practice rapidly, must nevertheless seek to adjust themselves as rapidly as possible; and the time-lag between the necessity of adjustment and the possibility of successful adjustment naturally contributed to the problems which they encountered. But in some areas they responded remarkably. The building of new churches and chapels to meet the new urban populations was a generous feat. The acceptance of evolutionary theory into Christian thought, and the adoption of the historical methods of Biblical criticism, were accompanied by pains but were substantially completed over thirty years.

We have seen that of these two great facts upsetting the Churches, the intellectual and the social, such evidence as exists points on the whole to the social as the more important of the two. This may be partly because a social influence is easier for the historians to test than an intellectual influence. But little signs point to it. In the 90s the country churchgoers were disturbed by Sunday golfers coming down from London and getting out of the train with their golf clubs just as the worshippers were on their way to church. Why? Was it merely that the development of trains and of golf-clubs made easy a way of Sabbath breaking which was hardly possible before, and neither urbanization nor intelligence had anything to do with it? Was it simply that the Sunday trains suddenly juxtaposed the incomparable customs of town and country? Or had the customs of the town changed, either because it was a larger town than it used to be, or because being larger it inevitably contained more people who did not accept any duty of churchgoing? Or had the duty of churchgoing weakened in the town because newspapers and books and conversation made known ideas which challenged the basis on which the duty of churchgoing rested? Or was it nothing but a mysterious and irrational change of social custom, like the increase of hair on men's faces after the Crimean war, or like the death of the belief that clergymen should not go to theatres?

We hear of men who hesitated to take orders in the Church of England, or to accept a pastorate in one of the Free Churches—among the latter, William Hale White (Mark Rutherford) is pre-eminent. Victorian critics were inclined to declare that "many men" were deterred from taking orders by their inability to profess what the Church insisted that they profess. Of course men had always been deterred from taking orders by this inability. It is easier to find general assertions that more men found it difficult during the second half of the reign of Queen Victoria than to find instances of men who found it difficult and told men why. These assertions are particularly common during the earlier 60s, when men argued over Colenso and the historical truth of the Old Testament, and during the 90s when they argued over miracle. Mrs Humphry Ward constructed one of the most famous of Victorian novels, *Robert Elsmere*, about a clergyman who must resign his parish because he could no longer believe and teach what he was expected to believe and teach. The individual loss of faith perhaps most momentous in its consequences, that of Leslie Stephen, dated from the earlier 60s. The future statesman C. F. G. Masterman would have liked to take orders in the 90s, and yet found an obstruction in his mind, arising from the difficulties of historical knowledge. Though we cannot find many instances, we do find a few to illustrate the general assertion that in the 60s and 90s intellectual travail prevented some from taking orders who on every other ground, *ex hypothesi*, would have wished to do so.

However, the statistics of those taking orders do not confirm at all points this view of the matter. It is true that the numbers, which rose unsteadily, reached their maximum in 1886 and then turned downwards; and they thus far confirm the supposition that the intellectual troubles of the 90s had their effect. But if this turn downwards rested solely upon the intellectual argument we should expect an even more remarkable turn downwards during the 60s, when the intellectual argument was much more exciting and caused far more turmoil among Christians. On the contrary, the number of persons ordained during the 60s continued (on the whole) to rise; and an examination of the quality of the candidates does not suggest that the rise of the 60s was achieved by opening the doors to candidates not qualified intellectually. The percentage of graduates (confessed to be an imperfect test of intellectual qualifications) remained sufficiently stable. When therefore we are told that "men do not take orders nowadays because they are compelled to profess what they cannot believe", we need to make quite sure that the assertion is not made by a liberal who wishes the Church to adjust itself more rapidly to modern knowledge as he (the liberal) conceives that it ought to adjust itself, and that the fall in numbers is not the cause of the assertion rather than the other way round.

When, therefore, the fall in ordinands was at last observed, we must also take into consideration some of the following: the level of tithe; the expansion and respectability of professions like teaching and the civil service; the decline of the landed interest, of which many country parsons were formerly part; the extent to which bishops and other pastors talked publicly about the poverty of the clergy, in order to raise additional money for their support; the changing nature of the work, as so much of it became suburban and as the parishioners became less immobile. I do not say that these reasons, or any of them, account better for the turn downwards of ordinands than the intellectual unsettlement. But we need much more evidence before we can determine whether a social cause (like the level of stipend) was less important than an intellectual cause—such as, you must identify yourself with a Church which is regarded by some intellectuals as teaching what is not true.

Let us try to state another "social" cause, and see whether it takes us anywhere. "The churches were less central to the activities of the state in 1901 than in 1837." Putting a point to this proposition, we ask whether clergymen and ministers at the end of the reign were doing work more peripheral to society than similar ministers at the beginning of the reign; without wishing to define precisely what could be meant by "peripheral to society".

That great preacher Robertson of Brighton once wrote this:

> By the change of times the pulpit has lost its place. It does only part of that whole which used to be done by it alone. Once it was newspaper,

schoolmaster, theological treatise, a stimulant to good works, historical lecture, metaphysics, etc., all in one. Now these are partitioned out to different officers, and the pulpit is no more the pulpit of three centuries back, than the authority of a master of a household is that of Abraham, who was soldier, butcher, sacrificer, shepherd, and emir in one person.[6]

As is evident from the sentence, Robertson was not contrasting the present time with the recent past but with the age of the Reformation. Yet the manner of the comparison suggests that he was aware of something beginning to happen in his own day. The country clergyman was once the only educated man in the village apart from the squire and perhaps a farmer or two. His parishioners learnt their reading and their history as well as their religion and morals out of the Bible. What he said was instruction *de haut en bas*. The clerical handbooks of the earlier part of the reign assume that the pulpit is a place where the parish will gain knowledge and recommend the parson to take much time in preparing his sermon because it is so important to the parishioners. The town parson at the end of the reign was one educated man among many. His words were the words of an equal, to be weighed and discussed. He must convince more by reasoning than by authority. Rather than communicating to men a truth which they were supposed to accept passively, he must lead them onward to search out the truth for themselves.

The symbol of this was the creation of a national system of education and the consequent diminution of the clergyman's part in the total scheme of education. Many parish priests continued to take an important part in the religious education of the country. But, even where the schools were church schools in a formal sense, they were almost always receiving taxpayers' money for their support, and they were no longer the parson's private and personal school in quite the way in which they started. More momentous than the grants of Government money was the consequent development of the profession of teachers. In the days of Dr Arnold it had not been quite "respectable" to be a teacher unless one was also a clergyman. It was not a profession which a "gentleman" considered entering. After 1870 the lingering remains of this feeling rapidly disappeared. Though many clergymen were still schoolmasters, the profession lost its particular link with the clergy as education in England broadened out and became lay.

The people of England, as their rate of literacy rose, were able to support, and be further educated by, an expanding number of newspapers, a few national but most of them either local or in some way vocational. The best of these provincial newspapers, like the *Manchester Guardian* or the *Birmingham Daily Post,* were of the highest quality in journalism, and treated religion with sympathy and understanding. At the opposite extreme were sheets intended to propagate some perhaps fierce brand of dogma, theistic or otherwise. There is little doubt that the expansion of the press made the people of England sit a little more detachedly to religious commitment. It is not quite clear why that should be so, nor is it easy to find evidence to illustrate such a growth in detachment. In a manner the press was situated like the Government. It was dealing with a mixed population, which corporately could apprehend only simple issues. An editor from Birmingham, who was a staunch member of a Church, urged the Church of England to face the fact that the newspapers could not but be neutral among the Churches nowadays. This relative neutrality in newspapers of wide circulation did not mean that specially religious newspapers were wanting. The expansion of the press included an enormous proliferation of religious newspapers or magazines intended for the parish, the town, the congregations, or the ministers. Parish magazines date from the 60s. But, though several attempts were made to found a "national" newspaper of a specially religious kind, no such attempt succeeded.

A similar move away from the central control of society was the rapid decline, especially after 1872, in the number of clerical magistrates. At the end of the century there were still a few clerical magistrates, but the number diminished through the reign. The axiom that something of incongruity rested upon the clerical magistrate became so commonly held that there was a little jolt of surprise when a modern scholar (Dr Kitson Clark) pointed out how natural and how public-spirited was the link between clergyman and magistrate during the earlier part of the Victorian age. Later Victorian clergymen themselves felt something inappropriate, as though the office must be a barrier to those social encounters with the poor, the delinquent, and the ordinary folk which were seen to be their special work.

In this sense the Christian minister again became a little less engaged with the government of society. But it would be erroneous to see in this change of custom any part of the process that might be called "secularization". The clergymen became a little less involved in the governmental structure of the country, but no less involved with the people of the country.

In just the same way the incumbent was formerly chairman of the vestry and therefore *ex officio* the chairman of the local government of the village. In towns his official place in local government vanished much earlier. In the country it nominally remained until 1894, or nearly all the reign. For in 1894 the Local Government Act separated the secular government from the vestry and left the incumbent and his churchwardens with no *ex officio* status upon the new parish council—though of course they might be elected to it. Some people said at the time that this act was a subtle way of disestablishing the Church of England. This view of the act was absurdly exaggerated. For the incumbent, if he were a good man, continued to play a very important part in village affairs, after as before. And long before 1894 the powers of the vestry had been whittled away almost to vanishing. The real government of the village lay with various authorities created at various times, from county councils to highway boards. The vestry, as a secular body, had become an anachronism and the act of 1894 was tardy in recognizing the need for something new.

It is not easy, then, to establish that Christian ministers were any less central to the activities of the society, except in two main respects, both of which had far-reaching consequences:

1. Clergymen in villages were inevitably more central to the life of their society than clergymen in towns—but at the beginning of the reign England was largely a rural society and at the end of the reign England was largely an urban society. In a big town Christian ministers often played a big part in public life, sometimes a leading part. But they might be ministers of any denomination, and the part which they played often rested more upon their personal qualities than their office.

2. By the end of the reign Christian ministers were no longer the chief agents in promoting and maintaining the schools to educate the mass of the English population. Nor were the ancient universities, as formerly, linked constitutionally with the Church of England. Education, like history and science, established its independent rights apart from the Churches; though the overwhelming majority of the country believed that any education worth the name must include religious education.

Now try this proposition: Christian ministers were less influential in the society of 1901 than in the society of 1837; meaning by society Society.

The Anglican clergyman of 1837 was very influential with the upper class because he was so often himself a member of the upper class, the squire's younger brother, the peer's younger son. It was a vocation of public spirit which a young man might undertake. Fifty years later such younger sons usually went into other professions, army or civil service or even business. The most remarkable illustration of this is the different attitude of the squire and the Church towards private patronage, illustrated in the two parliamentary reports on the question of 1874 and 1880; which yet show enough conservatism to make it clear that many members of the upper class still valued this mode of "placing" their sons in a work which both befitted their station and benefited local society.

This is so easy to caricature—and a number of Victorians, from Anthony Trollope downwards, were quick to caricature it—that we shall be in danger of smiling and underestimating the importance of the change in the trend towards "secularization". Canon Stanhope in *Barchester Towers* certainly did less to maintain the influence of the Church of England than the poorest curate in the County of Barset. And yet good men during the 60s and 70s—men like Professor Stubbs or Bishop Samuel Wilberforce—for no merely external reasons regretted that the idea of a *clergyman* was slowly being prised away from its almost necessary connection with the idea of a *gentleman*; merely because the town parishes needed far more clergymen than the leisured classes were able or willing to supply. They could not point to any particular evidence, except the datum of much experience (though far from all experience, as the quite contrary evidence of the lesser Independent chapels proves) that the uneducated were helped more by an educated minister than by one uneducated. They had a sense that the link between Church and the leisured classes was being weakened and that this must diminish the general influence of the Church in society. If, however, good men held this opinion, there were other good men who held quite the opposite. Hurrell Froude called the opinion the "gentleman-heresy" and had many successors who were equally contemptuous. This view of Froude won the argument because events were upon its side; and by the 90s it seemed to be an opinion held only by nostalgic conservatives. Before we dismiss it, we should remember that to the end of his life Cardinal Manning longed for Roman Catholic priests, so many of whom were Irish, to acquire the standing in society which came naturally to the Anglican clergymen. He thought that his priests were shut up in the sacristy and could never come out to influence ordinary life until their place in English society was more assured.

We need more local studies of religious development. A mass of local evidence lies awaiting investigation, though it is not easy to assess when it is collected. We have valuable studies of Camberwell by H. J. Dyos and Sheffield by E. R. Wickham and Liverpool by R. B. Walker, and good work has also been done in two unpublished Cambridge theses, on Birmingham by D. E. H. Mole and on Leicester (and Leicestershire) by D. M. Thompson. The Victoria County Histories have helped, especially over Birmingham and the city of York. The impact of this and other evidence at present is a bewildering local variety, and a sense of the uniqueness of each area of England rather than the common influences affecting the whole society. At the moment our need is rather to see the religious issues of the individual city or its countryside as they changed through the Victorian years. Sooner or later we must work back in an attempt to define, with rather less hesitation, the common influences.

NOTES

1. G. W. E. Russell, *Arthur Stanton*, p. 43.
2. Peel Papers, British Museum Add. Mss 40499, 144, 146.
3. Beatrice Webb, *My Apprenticeship*, pp. 258–9.
4. *Life*, p. 98.
5. *Life*, p. 303.
6. Brooke, *Life of F. W. Robertson* (new ed. 1873), ii, p. 54.

6

The Prayer Book in the Victorian Era

R. C. D. JASPER

It has often been assumed that, once the Book of Common Prayer was restored in 1662, little or nothing was done to disturb or dispute its control over the public worship of the Church of England until the present century. This is simply not true. The Prayer Book of 1662 indicated a rejection of Presbyterian schemes for comprehension: but rejection is not the same as liquidation, and from the late seventeenth century onwards agitation to revise the Prayer Book in this direction continued unabated. Indeed, in 1689 one set of proposals even reached Convocation, only to meet with defeat at the hands of Tory High Church members of the Lower House. These schemes usually included such elements as the omission of references to priestly absolution, the replacement of the canticles by psalms, the removal of the Athanasian Creed, and the relaxation of rules requiring the use of the surplice, kneeling for the reception of Communion, and the sign of the Cross in Baptism. At the same time it must be remembered that High Churchmen disliked the idea of change; and a love of the Prayer Book was a notable trait in the growing body of Evangelicals. Then, with the coming of the French Revolution at the end of the eighteenth century, all suggestion of reform for a time vanished. The violence of the Revolution produced in England a reaction, engendering a general attachment to the institutions of Church and State as representative of law, order, and security. Dissenters were regarded with suspicion and distrust, and a fear of papal aggression was enough to cause panic and alarm.

But this loyalty to and affection for the Establishment was short-lived. Once the war with France was over in 1815, the reformer again came into his own, and there was little that he did not wish to touch. The removal of abuses was not enough: customs and institutions must be done away simply because they were old—and here the Church of England was easy prey. In 1828 the Test and Corporation Acts were repealed; in 1829 Roman Catholics were emancipated; and then came the Parliamentary Reform Act of 1832, episcopal opposition to which only made the Church more unpopular. William Palmer gave a graphic description of the situation:

> It was then that we felt ourselves assailed by enemies from within and from without. Our prelates insulted and threatened by ministers of state—continual motions made for their expulsion from the legislature—demands for the suppression of Church-voters, on the avowed principle of opening the way for a total separation of Church and State—clamours loud and long for the overthrow of the Church—Dissenters and Romanists triumphing in the prospect of its subversion, and assailing it with every epithet calculated to stimulate popular hatred.[1]

Who were these enemies from within? People like Lord Henley with his *Plan of Church Reform* in 1832 and Dr Arnold with his *Principles of Church Reform* in 1833, who in their proposals included changes in the Liturgy which followed the familiar pattern of the previous century. Nevertheless, even professedly loyal elements in the Church were not entirely averse to change. The High Church magazine *The British Critic* accepted the principle that it would be wrong to assume that the Prayer Book was incapable of change or improvement and admitted that such elements as the Damnatory Clauses in the Athanasian Creed did trouble many consciences.[2] The Evangelical journal *The Christian Observer* made the same point, adding that the Church, with all her faults, was well worth reforming:[3] while Connop Thirlwall, one of the great and learned Liberal Churchmen of the century, wrote in 1832:

> Among the things most indispensably requisite to the stability of the Church of England, I hold to be a revision of her Liturgy . . . Many persons are driven out of the communion of the Church by their repugnance to its liturgical form, a repugnance springing from the purest and most enlightened conviction.[4]

Pioneers in this move for liturgical change were William Winstanley Hull, a barrister, and the Venerable Edward Berens,

Archdeacon of Berkshire, who published pamphlets in 1828, described by *The British Critic* as "pilot balloons", sent up to ascertain the movement of popular feeling. Reaction was favourable, and they marked the beginning of a stream of pamphlets which developed into a flood and continued for the rest of the century. The schemes produced between 1828 and 1840 largely followed a uniform pattern:

1. The removal of lessons from the Apocrypha and of passages which were distasteful or unedifying.
2. An abridged fusion of the three morning services.
3. The omission of the Athanasian Creed, or at least of its Damnatory Clauses.
4. A modification of passages referring to priestly absolution and baptismal regeneration.
5. A modification of the marriage service on the grounds of delicacy.

Some of the criticisms which were voiced still have a familiar ring today. Note, for example, the remarks of the Reverend John Riland of Yoxall in 1832:

> What do we gain by the . . . ill selection of Proper Lessons, Epistles and Gospels: the retention of legendary names and allusions in the Calendar, . . . the repetitions of the Pater-noster, Kyrie Eleison, and Gloria Patri; the wearisome length of the Services; the redundance and assumptions of the State Prayers; . . . the discordance between the Prayer Book and Bible translations of the Psalms.[5]

Now most of these schemes were little more than "scissors and paste" types, relying very little on any extensive liturgical knowledge. In fact, during this period the scientific study of liturgy in this country was virtually non-existent. Nevertheless, some of the ideas expressed were by no means devoid of merit and were worthy of consideration.

1. Many realized the necessity of revising those elements in the Prayer Book which were either out-of-date or no longer understood. The same view has been expressed admirably nearer our own day by Miss Evelyn Underhill:

> Institutional Religion has, as à Kempis says, an eye that looks on Eternity and an eye that looks on Time. . . . Carrying and expressing our little human love of the Abiding, it is itself conditioned by the law of change; and perpetually brings into touching association the

> unchanging Majesty of God and the changing insights and desires of men, with their close dependence on the life of sense . . . Thus our Book of Common Prayer must be the Book both of a living and of a historic society.[6]

2. Many grasped the important fact that the revision of the Prayer Book involved liturgical experiment. Forms of worship can only be assessed in the light of experience; and their development can only be gradual. New liturgy cannot be evolved solely around a table: it must depend in some measure on what is *done* within the congregation and on one's knees.

3. Some realized that changes in the Prayer Book should also involve a modification in the relations between Church and State. So Archbishop Whately of Dublin pointed out in 1840 that the Church should have freedom to order her own forms of worship, for the State was not really a body competent to deal with such spiritual matters.

In the face of this agitation for reform, the Prayer Book was strongly defended by the Tractarians. They had no desire to tamper with it in order to comprehend Dissenters or to ease tender consciences. On the contrary they demanded a return to its original ideals, convinced that in it the Church of England possessed a worthy foundation-stone of all its faith and practice. Meetings were held; local defence associations were formed; and an address was presented to the Archbishop of Canterbury in February 1834 expressing "deep-rooted attachment to that venerable Liturgy, in which she [the Church] has embodied in the language of ancient piety the Orthodox and Primitive Faith", and deprecating the restless desire for change.[7] Other addresses followed; and it became clear that there was considerable support for maintaining the Prayer Book as it stood. Among the *Tracts for the Times*, Tract 3 by Newman and Tract 4 by Keble defended the Book against change; Tracts 38 and 41 by Newman pleaded for loyalty to it: Tract 9 by Froude, Tract 43 by Thomas Keble, and Tract 75 by Newman opposed the shortening of church services; John Keble defended the Lectionary in Tract 13, the Athanasian Creed in Tract 22, and the Baptism and Marriage Services in Tract 40; while Newman defended the Burial Services in Tract 3. Other Tracts upheld the doctrines involved in the various Prayer Book services—priestly absolution, baptismal regeneration, the Real Presence, and the eucharistic sacrifice. John Keble also defended the Prayer Book in a number of poems in *Lyra Apostolica*. So, for example, the concluding poem, "The Remnant", referred to the angels who, although departing in the face of reform, promised not to forsake those who remained faithful to the Prayer Book.

> We go, but faithful hearts will find us near,
> Who cling beside their Mother in her woes,
> Who love the rites that erst their fathers loved,
> Nor tire of David's hymn, and Jesus' prayer:
> Their quiet altars, whereso'er removed,
> Shall clear with incense sweet the unholy air;
> In persecution safe, in scorn approved,
> Angels, and He who rules them, will be there.[8]

The Tractarians not only defended the Prayer Book but also demanded loyalty to it: services should not be mangled and adapted, and rubrics should not be ignored. When, however, they urged the restoration of what they claimed to be genuine Prayer Book worship, voices were raised in opposition. In May 1843 John Wilson Croker wrote a learned article on Ritualism in *The Quarterly Review*. First he referred to certain "novel usages" which were being introduced by people whom he called rubricians, or ultra-rubricians—not lawless men, but people who were standing for the law. Such usages were daily services, the use of the Prayer for the Church Militant when there was no communion, preaching in a surplice, the use of credence tables, and the administration of baptism during divine service. Then he went on to discuss what he called "fooleries"—altar candles, even unlit; bowing to the east or to the altar; and the eastward position of the celebrant at holy communion. Such practices were to be deplored. Bishops' Charges took the line that the Tractarians were not being lawless, but were fussily and needlessly reviving usages which were technically and legally right in themselves but had fallen into disuse. Archbishop Howley gave a lead when he addressed a Pastoral Letter to the clergy and laity of the Province of Canterbury in January 1845, in which he gave somewhat conventional advice in favour of obedience to the law and rubric, and yet at the same time defended those who followed customary usage rather than rubric.[9]

One result of this development was the series of court cases on ritualism, beginning with Westerton *v.* Liddell *re* St Barnabas, Pimlico, in March 1854. The decisions given proved to be of little value in deciding what was lawful and what was not lawful: for if judgement was given against the ritualists they simply refused to accept the findings of the secular courts on church matters and adopted a policy of passive resistance. It was one thing to bring a test case to find out what the law really was: it was another to try to compel obedience to the law. So the Evangelical journal *The Record* finally admitted in 1884:

> Ecclesiastical litigation is not only undesirable, but extremely likely to do mischief in the cause of Evangelical truth. We can hardly imagine any course more certain to prejudice public opinion against the party who pursue it, more inevitably doomed to failure so far as practical result is concerned, or more calculated to deaden spiritual vitality and promote a harsh and unchristian spirit.[10]

A second result of Tractarian action was a further spate of pamphlets urging that, if these men could find support for their "innovations" in the Prayer Book, then the Liturgy simply must be changed.

> These men have directed our attention to that specific portion of our formularies upon which alone any warrant for such designs can be founded; and where the need of alteration is therefore most urgent. And it is not too much to say that it has become not only an act of justifiable self-protection, but also a duty which we owe to Scriptural truth and Christian liberty, to demand some modification of that portion of the Liturgy upon which these pretensions are made to rest.[11]

This agitation was also fostered from 1859 onwards for some twenty years by a small but noisy and wealthy society called The Association for Promoting a Revision of the Book of Common Prayer[12] led by Lord Ebury, which laid down a programme of reform very much in line with that urged from 1689 onwards.

Meanwhile, in the 50s, new and important factors emerged which were destined to have some effect on the liturgical life of the Church. The first was the Religious Census, which was taken on Sunday, 30 March 1851. Those in charge of church services on that day were asked to count the heads of worshippers, morning and evening, and estimates were made of those who attended church twice or more, and those who were prevented from attending. The methods of calculation were regarded by some judges as unreliable and the figures have been questioned. Nevertheless the overall picture is fairly reliable. Despite the fact that the nation was regarded as basically Christian, with quite a high standard of churchgoing, the Census revealed that of nearly eighteen million people in England and Wales, only 7,260,000 had attended some service: while 5,290,000 could have attended some service but didn't. Some people clearly had good reason for not attending Church—they lacked proper clothes, they lived too far away from a place of worship, or they were deterred by the system of pew-appropriation; but the main reason appears to have been a lack of knowledge of or contact with the Christian Church. Not that this was entirely the fault of the clergy: what could a man do when given a parish of tens of thousands of people in a new industrial area? At this time the parish of Bradford, for example, contained some seventy thousand souls: and the Census did, in fact, indicate that the most obvious absentees were the urban working class, and especially those who lived in the new centres of industry.

These facts came to light just when the Convocations resumed their active functions for the first time since 1689, thanks largely to the efforts of Bishop Samuel Wilberforce. On 1 February 1854 the Convocation of Canterbury appointed a Joint Committee to consider whether the increase and conditions of the population did not render some adaptation of the Church's rules needful, to meet their spiritual necessities. The Sunday morning service was a typical example of the problem. Legally it was a combination of Mattins, Litany, and Holy Communion, to follow the one after the other. The practice had largely fallen into disuse, and the practice of early celebrations of the Holy Communion was growing. But there was no official recognition of these developments. As Bishop Wilberforce remarked about the early celebration, permission to have it was only "by tacit connivance". Then again there was a growing need for a second Sunday evening service, since it was the customary practice to have Evensong on Sunday afternoons.

The Joint Committee reported in July 1854 and proposed that, while the Prayer Book itself should remain unchanged, certain modifications might be made, of which the following were the most significant:

1. The Sunday morning service should be permissible as three separate entities.

2. On weekdays there should be a shorter form of Morning and Evening Prayer.

3. Occasional services from various Prayer Book materials should be permitted.

4. An authoritative selection of psalms and hymns should be produced.

This Report was one of the first official documents produced by the Convocations for nearly 200 years: and, though in some ways it was momentous, its fate was unfortunate. Opposition to any reform was expressed in no uncertain terms in the Lower House and the matter was allowed to drop.[13] It is interesting to note, however, that discussion on the necessity of the Church to apply itself to the needs of the "unchurched millions" tended to be confused on two basic issues. In the first place no one appeared to be very clear as to the precise people for whom new forms of service were intended—the non-churchgoers or the regular attenders. Secondly, there was no clear policy as to how liturgical change might be effected, although many recognized the importance of trying to avoid parliamentary action. In January 1860 a further Joint Committee suggested special lessons and prayers for such occasions as Harvest, National Humiliation, and National Thanksgiving, together with a "preaching service" composed basically of a sermon and prayers. These forms might be issued simply by royal authority, rather like State services. Once again, however, the opposition was too strong and the proposals were dropped.[14] In the following year Dr Pellew, Dean of Norwich, tried again, proposing that a Royal Commission might be appointed to consider how the Prayer Book might be adapted to the needs of the Church. But his attempt met with a similar fate: and in the face of opposition from his fellow clergy he withdrew his motion.[15]

While the official bodies of the Church dithered, what was happening at parish level? There were, of course, riots and disorders in a number of places in consequence of ritualistic innovations. But the general pattern of public worship was gradually changing. Services—and especially communion services—were held more frequently; there was an increasing use of organs and choirs; sermons became shorter but much more frequent; and congregations became more vocal. In this they were helped by a rapid replacement of metrical psalms by new hymnody. In the middle of the century new hymnals were appearing at a rate of rather more than one a year, and in 1861 there came the crowning achievement of the first edition of *Hymns Ancient and Modern*. The change is reflected in a remarkable statement by Archbishop Tait, himself no lover of ritualism, when presiding over a meeting of the Diocesan Church Building Society in August 1874:

> [The laity] may remember that many things to which they were perhaps accustomed in old times are remains of an age when great apathy prevailed, and they must be prepared not only for improvements in the outward appearance of the Church, but also in the services. I suppose there is no one of my age here but looks back with a

kind of shame to the sort of sermons that were preached, the sort of clergyman that preached them, the sort of building in which they preached them, and the sort of psalmody with which the service was ushered in; and, remembering these, I am perfectly astonished that the whole of the attachment of the people to the Church did not evaporate. But if all improvements had been resisted we should not have been where we are now.[16]

Then again, some attempts were made to reach the "unchurched millions". A typical pioneer was the Rev. J. C. Miller, the Evangelical Rector of Birmingham, 1848–60, who not only encouraged regular evening communion and breaking up the Sunday morning service into separate entities, but also engaged in open-air preaching. Then in 1855 Lord Shaftesbury succeeded in securing a modification of the law which had prohibited the meeting for religious worship of more than twenty people in any building except a church or a licensed dissenting chapel. This question had been a matter of debate for some time; and as early as 1833 Bishop Sumner of Winchester had declared in a Charge that he did not consider cottage readings or lectures as an infringement of the Act of Uniformity. But Shaftesbury's success was followed by a remarkable experiment in evangelism. Simple Sunday evening services for the non-churchgoer were held in Exeter Hall, London, in the summer of 1855, and they were attended by thousands of people, to the great delight of Bishop Tait. Unfortunately, they were soon inhibited by the Vicar of St Michael's, Burleigh Street, in whose parish the hall was situated, in spite of strong remonstrances from the Bishop and Lord Shaftesbury. They were, however, resumed soon afterwards by the nonconformists, while the Anglicans sought alternative accommodation elsewhere. Seven theatres in the poorest part of London were then rented, and the Sunday evening services held in these buildings met with immediate success.

It was a strange sight; from floor to ceiling the vast house was thronged; in boxes, stalls, pit, and gallery were costermongers, street cadgers, and labourers, women in fluttering rags, many with babies in their arms, boys in shirt-sleeves and corduroys, young men and maidens in their gaudy Sunday best. The people listened with extraordinary attention, as if they had never heard of the subject before.[17]

This effective venture soon had repercussions elsewhere. Westminster Abbey began Sunday evening services in 1858 and St Paul's Cathedral shortly afterwards. In both places the shortcomings were painfully obvious—the buildings were cold, the acoustics were deplorable, and the choice of preachers often unfortunate—but the crowds continued to come. The popular Sunday night service became an established fact.

This development owed much to the courage and enterprise of the Evangelicals; but there were other equally effective ventures which owed much to the Tractarians and Anglo-Catholics. Newman had helped to break new ground, both in liturgical knowledge as well as aids to devotion, when he provided extracts from the Roman Breviary in English in Tract 75: other developments soon followed. *The British Critic* pointed out in April 1840:

> The Liturgies of Rome and Paris were, till very recently, sealed books to the Protestant world. We well remember that when Bishop Lloyd began his lectures, twelve years since, it was hardly possible even to procure copies of them . . . But now Mr. Parker of Oxford finds it worth while to import a considerable number of copies both of the Roman and Parisian Breviaries every year; whence we infer . . . that the ancient Services are coming to be studied, not merely as a matter of literature, but for purposes of private devotion.[18]

From the middle of the century there appeared a growing number of devotional books, claiming to be complementary to the Book of Common Prayer, providing material drawn largely from the Roman Missal and Breviary, often couched in flowery language described by C. S. Lewis as medieval excess. Perhaps one of the best known of these books was *Catholic Prayers for Church of England People* which appeared in 1880 with a Preface by Fr A. H. Stanton, containing an English translation of the Roman rite, the Rosary, the Litany of the Sacred Heart, and other devotions. Such books often went out of their way to deny any charge of disloyalty to the Prayer Book. Orby Shipley's *Ritual of the Altar*, which appeared in 1870, stated in its preface:

> If it were permissible for the compilers of the English use in the sixteenth century to adopt materials from the Roman Missal for public recitation, it cannot be disloyal to take advantage of the same materials for the private edification of members of the same Church in the nineteenth century.[19]

At the same time, it must not be thought that Anglo-Catholics were simply content to use the 1662 Prayer Book with unofficial additions and alterations. From time to time proposals for revision were put out: and for the most part these followed the line of a return to the pattern of the 1549 Prayer Book, or a recovery of certain pre-Reformation elements which would have added richness and variety to prayers and lessons. Notable among the compilers of such proposals were J. M. Neale and R. F. Littledale—the former writing a series of articles in *The Ecclesiologist* in 1860 under the initials "H.S.L."[20] and the latter addressing an open letter to the Archbishop of Canterbury entitled *Catholic Revision* at the time of the appointment of the Royal Commission on Ritual in 1867. As may be expected, their proposals were very different from those of Lord Ebury and his friends and were argued on much more scientifically liturgical lines. Significant among their suggestions were:

1. The removal of the penitential opening to morning and evening prayer and the substitution of seasonal sentences.
2. Increased provision of special psalms, lessons, and prefaces for holy days.
3. An extension of canticles, and occasional prayers and thanksgivings.
4. The reconstruction of the eucharistic canon on 1549 lines.
5. The restoration of oil in baptism, confirmation, and the visitation of the sick.
6. The introduction of a form of compline with one variable lesson as a "third service".

Whether such a Prayer Book would have met with general acceptance in the Church of England at large is doubtful, but it would have certainly produced a more colourful book. And whatever criticisms might be levelled at the Anglo-Catholics and their "ritualistic" practices there is not the slightest doubt that they brought a new sense of reverence and dignity to public worship, and they also gave an element of warmth, beauty, and colour to the lives of many people living in rather dreary surroundings. So, for example one of Fr Lowder's assistants described the Sunday morning eucharist at St Peter's, London Docks, in 1860:

> I suppose there is not a more beautiful service in London or England than the High Celebration at St Peter's, London Docks . . . Besides the ennobling feeling thus engendered by a service offered willingly and not for money, the reverence and solemnity of the whole sacred act has had a surprising influence for good on the lives and tone of mind of those who took part in it. Indeed, this is the practical value of such a service, apart from its aspect towards God as our "bounden duty", that it raises the hearts of the poor out of the miseries of their earthly lot into the majesty and peace of heaven. The beauty and brightness of the services, the glorious music, the solemn dignity of the ritual, all these contrast with the squalidness and nakedness of

their homes, and make the church to them the very house of God, the gate of heaven. [21]

It was in the 50s and 60s of the nineteenth century, therefore, that the Church of England experienced considerable pressures for liturgical change—experiments in evangelistic forms of service, varied programmes for revising the Prayer Book, the production of supplementary books of devotion, the strong feelings aroused by ritualism, the need to reach the "unchurched" millions. There were frequent petitions to Parliamant to take action; and finally in 1867 a Royal Commission on Ritual was appointed to consider the differences of practice arising "from varying interpretations put upon the rubrics, orders and direction for regulating the course and conduct of public worship . . . and more especially with reference to the ornaments used . . . and the vestments worn . . .". The Commission produced four Reports—two dealing with the Ornaments Rubric, and recommending a restraint but not a total abolition or prohibition of the use of vestments, incense, and candles; and two more intimately concerned with the revision of the Prayer Book.

The Third Report, which appeared in 1870, dealt with the revision of the lessons appointed for Morning and Evening Prayer. The proposals were a marked improvement on the existing system and were rapidly adopted in a new Lectionary Measure. The old principle of "one lesson—one chapter" was abrogated in the interests of brevity and intelligibility, proper lessons on holy days were revised and extended, and a second set of Old Testament lessons for Sunday evenings was provided. It was a pity that special New Testament Sunday lessons were not included as well. Nevertheless, it was a notable advance that the needs of the layman who was normally a Sunday and not a weekday worshipper were recognized. Sunday and weekday cycles of lessons were now beginning to emerge as separate entities, which was wholly good. Furthermore, these proposals recognized the need of the Sunday "Third Service"—for the new set of Sunday lessons would be used either as alternative lessons at Evensong or as lessons for a "Third Service"; while at the Third Service the minister was given the freedom to choose his own second lesson from the Gospels. The Measure provided welcome relief and flexibility.

The Fourth Report, which also appeared in 1870, took the principle of flexibility considerably further and its proposals were finally incorporated in the Act of Uniformity Amendment Act or Shortened Services Act of 1872. This Measure did not effect any changes in the Prayer Book itself, but authorized the adaptation of its services to suit particular needs. Admittedly, simply from a liturgical point of view, its provisions left much to be desired. But when we remember that the scientific study of liturgy was still in its infancy, and that it did make a serious effort to face a missionary situation, there is much to be said in its favour. Indeed, many of its aims are still the aims of the Church today.

1. Provision was made for a shorter form of Daily Office on weekdays by allowing for one psalm, one lesson, one canticle and ending at the third collect.
2. The three elements of the "Morning Service" could be used as three separate entities, and the litany could be used at Evensong after the third collect.
3. On Sundays a "Third Service" could be used and its materials could be drawn from any part of the Prayer Book except the Communion Service.
4. Sermons could be preached apart from Divine Service.
5. On special occasions a minister could use a service composed of any materials in the Prayer Book and Bible provided he secured his Bishop's approval.

This Measure has often been criticized severely: but it would appear to have done considerable good. There is no doubt that it encouraged special services, such as Harvest Festivals, Lenten Devotions, and Compline,[22] while Sunday services took on a new lease of life, and particularly the use of the service of Holy Communion as an entity by itself. An interesting comparison can be shown from the records of the diocese of Winchester. In 1829, from a total of 319 parish churches, services were only held twice on a Sunday in 158, and elsewhere the norm was once; while Bishop Sumner urged each parish to aim at having Holy Communion once a month. But by 1899 Bishop Randall Davidson could report that only five churches were invariably closed from Sunday to Sunday, 182 churches had daily prayer all the year round, 320 churches were open daily for private prayer, 404 churches had Holy Communion at least once a week, and twelve churches had a celebration every day. Subsequently Randall Davidson, when Archbishop of Canterbury, pointed out that whereas cassocks, surpliced choirs, processional hymns, chanted psalms and the like had once been the cause of disturbance and even riot, by the end of the century they were widely accepted as normal.[23]

In the second half of the nineteenth century quite a revolution had taken place in the worship of the Church of England and there is no doubt that the trial of Edward King, the saintly Bishop of Lincoln, before Archbishop Benson in 1889, and the Judgment which followed in November 1890, took some of the sting from questions of controversy. As Archbishop Davidson remarked, "The effect was quieting on both clergy and laity, who felt that a good thing had been done properly." Throughout the changes the Book of Common Prayer had emerged intact: it was found that, with certain adaptations, it still worked. And although pleas for its reform in various ways were constant, the reformers only wished to make it—in their own eyes—a better book and more acceptable to other people. No one expressed the desire to cast it out altogether. But the realization was slowly dawning throughout the Victorian era that the liturgy was no static thing. It was an instrument, to be used by countless human souls in their approach to God: and as their situations changed, so had the instrument to be adapted accordingly. "It is for the Prayer Book to keep as close as may be to the living and growing soul of the Church; not for that living and growing soul to make a virtue of keeping close to a static book."[24] Thanks to the struggles of our forbears, we have come to accept this principle in our own day.

NOTES

1. W. Palmer, *A Narrative of Events connected with the Publication of the Tracts for the Times* (Oxford, 1843), pp. 2–3.
2. *The British Critic*, No. 12, pp. 303, 313; No. 23, pp. 294, 391–2; No. 25, pp. 43–5.
3. *The Christian Observer*, 1826, pp. 87, 600; 1833, p. 375.
4. J. J. S. Perowne and L. Stokes, *Letters Literary and Theological of Connop Thirlwall* (London, 1881), p. 104.
5. Quoted in A. P. Perceval, *A Letter to Lord Henley respecting his publication on Church Reform* (1832), pp. 4–5.
6. E. Underhill, "The Essentials of a Prayer Book", from *The New Prayer Book*, ed. by H. M. Relton (1927), pp. 50–1.
7. W. Palmer, *A Narrative of Events connected with the publication of the Tracts for the Times*, p. 95.
8. *Lyra Apostolica*, ed. H. C. Beeching (London, 1904), p. 125.
9. *Report of the Royal Commission on Ecclesiastical Discipline*, 1906, vol. 2, p. 346, sc. 12855.
10. *The Record*, 14 November 1884.
11. J. C. Fisher, *Liturgical Purity our Rightful Inheritance*, 1857, p. 90.
12. Later it became the Church Reform Society.
13. *Chronicle of the Convocation of Canterbury, 1847–57*, pp. 158–65, 174–8, 180–6, 196–8.
14. ibid., 1859–61, pp. 139–41, 152–65.
15. ibid., pp. 578–83, 615.
16. Quoted in A. B. J. Beresford Hope, *Worship in the Church of England*, 1874, p. 7.
17. E. Hodder, *The Life and Work of the Seventh Earl of Shaftesbury* (1886), vol. 3. p. 102.

18. *The British Critic*, April 1840, No. 54, p. 251.
19. Orby Shipley, *The Ritual of the Altar* (1870), p. xvii.
20. "H.S.L." were the second consonants of his two Christian names and surname–Jo*h*n Ma*s*on Nea*l*e.
21. Anon, *Charles Lowder* (1882), p. 167.
22. The Convocations themselves considered several forms from 1887 onwards.
23. *Report of Royal Commission on Ecclesiastical Discipline*, vol. 2, p. 388.
24. E. Underhill, from *The New Prayer Book*, p. 48.

INDEX